Animal Assisted Therapy
and the
Therapeutic Alliance
in the
Treatment
of
Substance Dependence

Martin Cortez Wesley Ph.D., LPCC, MAC

ISBN-13: 978-1475043204
ISBN-10: 1475043201

ABSTRACT

The purpose of this study was to evaluate the effect of animal assisted therapy (AAT) on the therapeutic alliance with an adult residential substance abuse population in group therapy. The question of whether a trained therapy animal can enhance the therapeutic alliance was recently posed by Fine and Mio (2006). In their call for additional research, they suggested that "the gold standard for research of this type is to have a random assignment to an AAT format and a traditional therapy format and then to determine which format led to a better therapeutic outcome" (Fine & Mio, p. 517). This quantitative study followed these recommendations by using randomized populations and controlled conditions to establish the effects of chosen variables that influence outcome. The study made comparisons of the mean differences between groups with and without the therapy dog. A one-way analysis of variance (ANOVA) was used to compute the mean differences and test the hypothesis for the efficacy of AAT. The results of the study indicate that the therapeutic alliance is enhanced with the addition of a therapy dog. The addition of a therapy dog also lowered heart and diastolic blood pressure rates. Population subgroups were assessed with mixed results. Clients seeking treatment for a dual diagnosis, clients with state social service involvement, and clients seeking treatment for alcohol did not verify the efficacy for AAT. Males; females; pet owners; court ordered clients; and clients seeking treatment for polysubstance, cannabis, and methamphetamine dependence all supported the hypothesis, verifying the efficacy for AAT. The implications for social change for the verified hypothesis are profound. First, addiction professionals can increase treatment success by adding this complementary evidence-based practice. Secondly, for those already using AAT in treatment, social change will transpire by verifying empirically what practitioners already suspected anecdotally; specifically, that therapy animals enhance treatment outcome.

DEDICATION

This research work is dedicated to Dawn Wesley, my wife, lover, helper, and friend. I also want to dedicate this research to all therapy dogs and their human handlers who bring hope, love, and companionship to thousands of individuals in various settings throughout the world.

CONTENTS

TABLE OF CONTENTS

LIST OF TABLES

LIST OF FIGURES

ACKNOWLEDGMENTS

I would like to acknowledge the help and support of my advisor, Dr. Sandra Rasmussen who guided me through the dissertation process, and to the other members of my dissertation committee, Dr. Stephanie Cawthon and Dr. Richard Waite.

I want to acknowledge Dr. Neresa Minatrea for her encouragement and consultation in the process and help in the treatment phase of this dissertation. Finally, this project could not have been possible without Mitzi Ann, Dr. Minatrea's four-legged companion.

I also could not have completed this project without the support and encouragement of my three daughters, Destiny, Brittany, and Danae; my parents, Reverend James Wesley and Norma Wesley; and my in-laws, Dr. Norman Fisher and Lois Fisher. I also want to acknowledge my own pet, Sadie Mae (the wonder weenie), a mini dachshund, that provides me stress reduction through comedy relief.

CHAPTER 1

INTRODUCTION TO THE STUDY

Introduction

Hundreds of studies and the historical accumulation of expert clinical opinion dating as far back as Freud's early research (1913) acknowledge the significant importance of how the therapeutic alliance determines treatment success (Meier, Barrowclough , & Donmall , 2005; Meier, Donmall, McElduff, Barrowclough, & Heller, 2006). Studies have consistently found that the quality of the therapeutic alliance relates to treatment outcome and, in fact, can be the most important variable contributing to therapeutic success or failure (Orlinsky, Ronnestad, & Wilutzki, 2003). Measurement of outcome success is different depending on the individual and population served. Sobriety is the desired therapeutic outcome for a substance-abusing client seeking recovery. The problem in all addiction treatment and research has been how to get clients to attach to and stay in treatment long enough for successful outcome. Studies confirm that enhancing the therapeutic alliance can increase sobriety rates for clients seeking treatment for their substance abuse problem (Miller, Taylor, & West, 1980; Connors, DiClemente, Carroll, Longabaugh, & Donoban, 1997).

In the past 40 years, animal assisted therapy (AAT) moved from their humble beginnings fringed with ridicule to a successful, research-based therapy (Hines, 2003). The professional community first overlooked AAT as a viable therapy for years (Arkrow, 1993) but is now a healthy and positive experience for most populations. AAT is not a specific technique but rather the therapy dog or other animal is an adjunct to the treatment process, helping to engage the client in the therapeutic program (Corson & Corson, 1978).

AAT can strengthen the therapeutic alliance in several ways. One way to use the therapy animal is as an interest topic to engage the client into verbal interactions. Additionally, the animal can reduce the client's anxiety about being in the therapist's office or in a group setting, making the client less resistant to the therapeutic intervention. The therapy animal does little but be itself, and has the client's trust well before the client trusts the human therapist (Chandler, 2005). Finally, if the client bonds with the animal as an adjunct to the therapeutic team, the client may be more committed to completing his or her therapeutic goals (Cieslak, 2001).

Keeping good morale in a residential substance abuse facility is important and can be the difference between patients who complete their treatment or those who go back to their old way of life. When a therapy dog comes to a residential substance abuse unit, morale improves. It can be very difficult for a client to admit to having a chemical dependency disorder and come to a strange facility to work on his or her problem. This scenario can lead to depression and anxiety, working against recovery, which they are seeking. Therapy dogs or other animals can help clients overcome this depression and anxiety associated with being in residential treatment (Bardill & Hutchinson, 1997; Campbell-Berg, 2000).

Many substance abuse treatment programs can become routine and rarely allow clients to leave the facility. Frequently, the patients attempt to cope with the loss of their independence and lack of family support. This can lead to clients becoming apathetic and angry, resulting in the client not getting the most of their treatment and eventually having higher rates of relapse (Reilly, Clark, & Shopshire, 1996). When a therapy dog visits the unit, boredom lifts, breaking up monotony for the client and staff as well. A person coping with the stress of residential or inpatient treatment may feel like his or her world is tumbling down around them, yet a pet animal remains constant. AAT can enhance the motivation, encouragement, inspiration, and insight properties of therapy. AAT improves retention and motivation for participation in therapy (Holcomb & Meacham, 1989). The animal needs a human to provide its basic life needs. Animals create mastery experiences for people through their submission to commands. A patient distressed from a substance abuse disorder or dual diagnosis may be forced to follow directions much of the time from facility staff, judges, drug court staff, probation or parole officers and others, yet they can still give commands and remain in charge of an animal (Beck & Katcher, 1996).

Psychological stress can contribute to drug and alcohol relapse (Brandy & Sonne, 1999). In animal studies, stress was the most powerful and reliable experimental manipulation that was used to induce a relapse (Haleem, 1996). Acute stress can bring on the fight-or-flight response, which elevates the heart rate and increases blood pressure. Traditional confrontational group therapy in drug and alcohol treatment centers has the potential for increasing stress levels and intensifying the chance of relapse, thus resulting in the therapeutic relationship being damaged (Miller, Rollnick, & Conforti, 2002).

Stressors do not need to be physical to create an increased need to take drugs or alcohol. According to Ramsey and Van Ree (1993), lab rats that witnessed another rat receiving physical discomfort increased self-administration for cocaine. Animals exposed to stressful situations such as being in an unfamiliar group of animals but protected from physical violence increased the possibility that the animal would use more alcohol or drugs (Piazza and Le Moal, 1998).

According to Yalom (2005), the first few group sessions can be very anxiety producing for the client. The client may experience a form of anxiety, which can help to motivate them in these initial group sessions. However, there are limits to the helpful qualities of anxiety. A client can be overtaken by the anxiety and be unable to function well in the group. An optimal degree of anxiety will help to motivate and increase alertness, but excessive anxiety will impede the client's ability to cope with the stress of the new situation. "In group therapy, crippling amounts of anxiety may prevent the introspection, interpersonal exploration, and testing of new behaviors essential to the process of change" (Yalom, p. 307). Treatment techniques that help lower stress, such as AAT, can play a pivotal role in successful addiction group therapy.

According to Bordin (1979), there are three elements of the therapeutic alliance: bonds, tasks and goals. Bonds involve the quality of the client-therapist relationship that involve trust, caring and mutual involvement. Tasks include dimensions to which the client and therapist are comfortable with the environment and activities in therapy. Finally, goals involve the extent to which the client and therapist are working toward mutual goals that benefit the client. AAT can affect each of these three elements of the alliance, measured through the scales of the HAQ-II. The measurement of vital signs (heart and blood pressure rates) can also help to measure stress and explore the tasks dimension of the therapeutic alliance.

Social support theory (Hupcey, 1998) and attachment theory (Flores, 2004) formed the basis for the theoretical perspective of this research project. Social support theory and attachment theory stress the positive health effect of human social companionship. These theories are interested in the positive effects of close neighborhoods, the benefits of marriage, church family or the positive effects of peer support. Animals are a source of social support and attachment for many individuals. Many people consider their pet as a "member of the family" or a confidant. Companion animals can also increase the frequency of human social contact (Eddy, Hart, & Boltz, 1988).

The human-animal attachment or bond is an affectionate, friendly, companionable interaction between an animal and a human (Messent & Serpell, 1981). Attachment is a social need required for the maintenance of a healthy well-being. Although attachment studies have typically examined human-to-human interaction, attachment to animals involves many of the same health benefits (Allen, Blascovich, Tomaka, & Kelsey, 2001; Odendaal, 1999, 2000).

Unfortunately, human-to-human relationships can be difficult due to multifaceted interdependent variables and human selfishness. In contrast, attachment to an animal can be mutual, reciprocal, and less complicated than human-to-human interactions (Rynearson, 1978). For some, the emotional support from an animal can have greater strength and stability than that of a human relationship. Human physical or emotional weakness will not damage animal-human relationships. Animals are available when called, nonjudgmental and predictable in their responses (Fine, 2000; Fine, 2006). Pet owners benefit from a greater sense of self when they perceive their pets as caring for and needing them regardless of how they perceive themselves. Finally, no special social learning skills need to elicit the attention of a therapy animal; however, human relationships are much more complicated.

Although attachment and relationships are important, the client does not necessarily need to bond to the animal to receive the benefits from AAT. Fish in tanks (Katcher, Segal, & Beck, 1984) and birds in communal cages (Beck, Seraydarian, & Hunter, 1986) can have a significant influence on health and well-being. According to Friedmann, Thomas, and Eddy (2000), three areas classify human responses to animal exposure: people explicitly looking at or observing animals or pictures of animals; people implicitly observing or being in the presence of animals; and people touching or interacting with animals.

Animals seem almost unaware of being able to perceive human inadequacies. Animals do not impose quality standards on their owners or judge them for their failures (Ross, 1983). Animals provide companionship, provide pleasurable activity, give individuals something to care for, help people feel safe, bring people to play and laugh, provide a source of constancy in people's changing world, are a stimulus to exercise, comfort with touch and are a pleasure to watch (Beck & Katcher, 1983).

Animals help fulfill a person's need to be wanted and have unconditional acceptance. Animals are loyal and nonjudgmental. According to Katcher and Friedmann (1980), there are nine healthy attributes pets bring to their owners and animals bring to clients in AAT or animal assisted activities, (AAA). These include companionship; pleasurable activity; facilitating exercise, play, and laughter; being something to care for and a source of consistency; allowing feelings of security; being a comfort to touch; and being pleasurable to watch. According to the literature, animals perform many roles to help the client accomplish specific therapeutic goals.

Everyone has a need for physical touch, for optimal physical and emotional growth (Spitz, 1950; Reite, 1989). Many substance-abusing clients have pushed their families and loved ones away for the comfort supplied by chemicals (McCrady & Hay, 1987). A code of distrust, selfishness, and conditional acceptance describes most of their relationships. Addiction and healthy interpersonal attachment are at opposite ends of the continuum. It is almost impossible for a practicing alcoholic or addict to fulfill the demands of healthy interpersonal relationships (Steinglass, 1987). Distrust, disappointments, inconsistencies, betrayal, and jealousy dominate most intimate relationships of substance abusers (Brennan, Moos, & Kelly, 1994). Developing new relationships or beginning a dialogue with strangers is difficult for most individuals but almost beyond the capacity for substance abusers without help. Substance abusers try to manage the uncertainties and difficulties of interpersonal relationships by escaping to temporary substitutes. Chemicals serve as a compensatory function, providing temporary emotional relief by helping lubricate this awkward situation and the incompetence in their interpersonal attachment styles (Flores, 2004).

The interpersonal skills substance abusers possess early in their use decline rapidly. Managing relationships becomes progressively complicated, leading to an increasing dependence on chemicals and hastened tumble in their personal life. Substance abusers will remain susceptible to replace one compulsive addiction for another until they abandon their dysfunctional attachment styles and develop the capability for healthy interpersonal relationships. Countless behavioral activities can be as obsessive and unmanageable as the client's drinking or drug use. They can become compulsive eaters, gamblers, internet gamers or use sex as they used substances to counteract the meaninglessness or life, anxiety, and depression that frequently threaten to overcome them (Flores, 2004).

Substance abusers usually enter treatment under extreme outside pressure from their families, employers, the court system, or due to acute health problems related to their chronic substance abuse (Smith & Meyers, 2004). Many alcoholics and addicts are antisocial and angry because circumstances and influential others in their lives have forced them into treatment which they feel they do not need or want (Diclemente, Bellino, & Neavins, 1999). Even when addicts and alcoholics agree that they need treatment, they usually embrace a secret desire to use chemicals in a non-addictive fashion, even though their past use illustrates that they cannot. Guilt and the desire to avoid legal and health consequences motivate compliance in treatment rather than a sincere desire to face their chemical problem. If alcoholics and addicts are not openly resistant and rebellious to treatment, they are working hard to create the impression of compliance so that they can meet whatever requirements expected of them and get back to their habitual patterns of dealing with life's demands and interpersonal relationships (Goldkamp, White, & Robinson, 2002). Active participation in the therapy process is required for successful treatment.

Animals help break this intimacy barrier and provide unconditional acceptance and love (Fine, 2000, 2006). Animals can also bring physical touch to the therapy session without breaking ethical boundaries. It is very difficult for a therapist to know when it is appropriate to physically touch a client. The therapist needs to avoid most physical touch in the therapy session so it is not misconstrued as grooming behavior or accidentally light the fire of passion between the therapist and client, leading to a charge of therapist incompetence (Koocher & Keith-Spiegel, 1998). Porous boundaries found with many addiction therapists who are in recovery themselves, intensify this concern (Bissell & Royce, 1987). Dogs are safe and can introduce therapeutic touch to the residential patient especially for those without other social support from family or friends. Therapy dogs work well as a surrogate for therapeutic touch when the client can benefit from nurturance and caring physical contract can offer (Chandler, 2005). Research to support this introduction is located in chapter 2.

Problem Statement

Substance abuse treatment is in need of complementary evidence-based treatment techniques and options that enhance the therapeutic alliance and reduce stress in therapy. AAT is a proven strategy for enhancing the therapeutic alliance with specific populations (Lefkowitz, 2005) and reducing stress (Allen et al. 2001). However, the literature reveals very little about how AAT can contribute to the treatment of individuals suffering from chemical dependency. Since most AAT is based on anecdotal success or limited or poor data (Barba, 1995; Garrity & Stallones, 1998; Wilson & Barker, 2003), empirical studies are needed to confirm these preliminary studies. . The question of whether a trained therapy animal can enhance the therapeutic alliance was recently posed by Fine and Mio (2006). In their call for additional research, they suggested that "the gold standard for research of this type is to have a random assignment to an AAT format and a traditional therapy format and then to determine which format led to a better therapeutic outcome" (Fine & Mio, p. 517).

The Background of this Study

The idea for this research evolved from watching female substance abuse residential clients care for stray cats from their smoking deck. The clients, separated from their own children or loved ones, appeared to be very caring toward the cats and kittens. The women were very protective of the cats when a staff member spoke of trapping and removing the animals. The male substance abuse clients also fed the squirrels and other wild animals, which came up to their smoking deck. The clients voiced to the researcher that they enjoyed the park setting in which the facility sat and how the squirrels and other park animals enhanced their residential stay. On occasion, staff members would bring their own pets to the facility only to see clients who would normally be withdrawn, openly express feelings of excitement and happiness to see the pet.

A resident pet within a substance abuse facility can present an opportunity for the residents to learn how to set and live with standards, behave consistently, and give rewards for good behavior. Their demeanor with the animals could be a place where they see how their behavior can affect all living creatures around them. When one is angry and yells around the animal, the animal may choose to leave. AAT interventions can teach clients lessons in building trust and on how to approach others in a nonthreatening manner. Residents can learn social skills such as the need to be gentle and to speak in a soft voice.

It is very difficult for an individual to leave their home and family for a therapeutic residential stay. Anything that can increase the enjoyment and satisfaction of a client's stay can help to reduce premature departures, allowing clients the full benefit of their therapeutic program. Animals can change a boring routine into a fascinating agenda. When watching these and other animal-human interactions among these clients, the researcher and manager of a substance abuse residential facility decided to conduct a research project to test the effectiveness of AAT with a community mental health, residential, substance abuse population.

The Purpose of the Study

The purpose of this study was to explore the relationship of AAT on the therapeutic alliance with an adult residential substance abuse population in group therapy. Numerous research studies have confirmed that the therapeutic alliance is a central component for treatment outcome and sobriety for the substance abuse client (Orlinsky, Ronnestad, & Wilutzki, 2003; Norcross, 2002). This study investigated the efficacy of using a trained therapy dog in a group setting to help facilitate the development and growth of the therapeutic alliance with clients in a residential substance abuse facility. Since a lack of empirical evidence exists relative to AAT

(Barba, 1995; Garrity & Stallones, 1998; Wilson & Barker, 2003), this is a quantitative study with experimental measures.

Further detail on the purpose of this study is in chapter 2 of this paper with a thorough literature review of the relevant topics.

Research Questions

1.   Does AAT make a positive difference in the therapeutic alliance as measured on the Helping Alliance Questionnaire (HAQ-II) for a sample of adult clients in residential substance abuse treatment in a group therapy session?

2.   Does AAT make a positive difference in lowering stress as measured by heart and blood pressure rates for a sample of adult clients in residential substance abuse treatment in a group therapy session?

Research Hypotheses

1.   Clients in an AAT group session will show higher ratings of the therapeutic alliance, as measured on the Helping Alliance Questionnaire (HAQ-II), over clients in a group therapy session without the therapy dog present.

2.   Client in an AAT group session will demonstrate lowered stress levels, as measured by lowered blood pressure (diastolic and systolic) and heart rate over clients in a group therapy session without the therapy dog present.

Detailed information on the design of this study is in chapter 3.

Theoretical Foundations

Animal Assisted Therapy (AAT)

The primary theoretical approach espoused for most AAT research is social support theory. This theory, originally developed to study the positive health effects of human social companionship, now includes the benefits of animal-to-human interaction. Just as human social networks such as family and marriage bonds, being part of a community of faith or being a member of a men's or women's support group can benefit the individual, so can the support provided by animals for their caregivers.

Social support theory is a multifaceted concept that is very difficult to define and measure. "Although this concept has been extensively studied, there is little agreement among theoreticians and researchers as to its theoretical and operational definition" (Hupcey, 1998, p. 1231). According to Stewart (1993), there is conceptual confusion among researchers' of what social support is and is not and little agreement among researchers of a working definition of the theoretical concept. Some researchers believe that the theoretical definitions of social support are too resistive and should remain somewhat vague because it is such a multifaceted concept. According to Vaux (1988, p. 28) "no single definition of social support will prove adequate because social support is a metaconstruct."

Attachment theory also provides a theoretical basis for the plethora of research evidence indicating that a good therapeutic alliance is the best predictor of successful therapy outcome. Attachment theory, with its emphasis on the importance of a secure attachment base, helps explain an important paradox about treatment; that secure attachment liberates. The alcoholic or addict's attachment to chemicals serves both as an obstruction and as a surrogate for interpersonal relationships. Before chemically dependent individuals attach to treatment, they must first get detached from the object of their addiction (Flores, 2004). Addicts and alcoholics will never develop healthy interpersonal attachments until they first surrender their addiction. Difficulty overcoming ineffective attachment styles (Ainsworth, 1989) can leave specific individuals vulnerable to addictive compulsions as compensatory behavior for their relational deficiency. These compulsive behaviors drive the addicts' inability to draw prolonged satisfaction from interpersonal relationships. Attachment theory holds that until substance abusers develop the capacity to establish mutually satisfying relationships, they remain vulnerable to relapse and addiction. To succeed in treatment, the addicted individual must learn how to establish healthy relationships (Flores).

The addict's inability to establish healthy relationships is a key factor in both the etiology and resolution of addictive disorders. Group psychotherapy, with its myriad of relationship possibilities provides a vehicle that not only reveals deficits in the individual member's attachment styles, but also furnishes a therapeutic culture that can be reparative in nature (Flores, 2004).

Social support theory and attachment theory, loosely defined in this section and expanded in chapter 2 of the literature review, serve as the foundation for this study. However, the results of the study will better define the theoretical concept of social support with the therapy animal and this specific population of adult substance dependent clients. This review also includes other theoretical concepts.

Definition of Terms

Addiction: For the purposes of this study, see substance dependence below.

Animal Assisted Activities: AAA provides opportunities for motivational, educational, recreational, and/or therapeutic benefits to enhance quality of life. Specially trained professionals, paraprofessionals, and/or volunteers, in association with animals that meet specific criteria, deliver AAA in a variety of environments. AAA is usually not goal-directed as is AAT (Delta Society, 1996).

Animal Assisted Therapy: AAT is a goal-directed intervention in which an animal is an integral part of the treatment process. Human service professionals with specialized expertise deliver AAT within the scope of practice of his or her profession. AAT attempts to improve a human's physical, social, emotional, and/or cognitive functioning. AAT is in a variety of settings including group or individual sessions (Delta Society, 1996). Other terms associated with AAT may include: pet therapy, pet psychotherapy, pet-facilitated therapy, pet-facilitated psychotherapy, four-footed therapy, animal assisted interventions, animal facilitated counseling, pet-mediated therapy, pet-oriented psychotherapy, companion-animal therapy and cotherapy with an animal (LaJoie, 2003; Kruger & Serpell, 2006).

Client, Patient, Resident: The words: client, patient, resident may be used interchangeably within this study to describe the individual subjects or groups of individuals contained in this study or to describe individuals or groups of individuals within other studies.

Handler: The handler refers to an individual who accompanies or is responsible for a dog that makes visits for providing therapy to individuals. For the purpose of this study, the handler is the primary therapist.

Human-Animal Bond: The human-animal attachment or bond is an affectionate, friendly, companionable interaction between an animal and a human (Messent & Serpell, 1981).

Resident Therapy Dog: The resident therapy dog is a full-time pet of a residential treatment program or nursing facility. Resident dogs are usually obedience trained and can enhance a residential program in many ways.

Researcher: The researcher in this project is the author of this research project. The researcher is not the therapist in the study.

Service Animal: A service animal means any guide dog, signal dog, assistance dog, hearing dog, mobility assistance dog or other animal individually trained to do work or perform tasks for the benefit of an individual with a disability. These services to the disabled could include guiding individuals with impaired vision, alerting individuals with impaired hearing to intruders or sounds, providing minimal protection or rescue work, pulling a wheelchair, or fetching dropped items (Department of Justice, 2002). Service animals are usually not pets. They are work dogs providing for the physical needs of their owners.

Substance Abuse or Chemical Abuse: The Diagnostic and Statistical Manual of Mental Disorders, Fourth Edition, Text Revision *(DSM-IV-TR,* APA, 2000) defines substance abuse as:

A. A maladaptive pattern of substance use leading to clinically significant impairment or distress, as manifested by one (or more) of the following, occurring within a 12-month period:

1. Recurrent substance use resulting in a failure to fulfill major role obligations at work, school, or home (e.g., repeated absences or poor work performance related to substance use; substance-related absences, suspensions or expulsions from school; neglect of children or household)

2. Recurrent substance use in situations in which it is physically hazardous (e.g., driving an automobile or operating a machine when impaired by substance use)

3. Recurrent substance-related legal problems (e.g., arrests for substance-related disorderly conduct)

4. Continued substance use despite having persistent or recurrent social or interpersonal problems caused or exacerbated by the effects of the substance (e.g., arguments with spouse about consequences of intoxication, physical fights)

B. The symptoms have never met the criteria for Substance Dependence for this class of substance (p. 199).

Substance Dependence or Chemical Dependence: The DSM-IV-TR, (APA, 2000) defines substance dependence as:

A maladaptive pattern of substance use, leading to clinically significant impairment or distress, as manifested by three (or more) of the following, occurring at any time in the same 12-month period: tolerance, as defined by either of the following:

1. Tolerance, as defined by either of the following:

   a. a need for markedly increased amounts of the substance to achieve intoxication or desired effect

   b. markedly diminished effect with continued use of the same amount of the substance

2. withdrawal, as manifested by either of the following:

      a.   the characteristic withdrawal syndrome for the substance (refer to Criteria A and B of the criteria sets for Withdrawal from the specific substances)

      b.   the same (or a closely related) substance is taken to relieve or avoid withdrawal symptoms

3.   the substance is often taken in larger amounts or over a longer period than was intended

4.   there is a persistent desire or unsuccessful efforts to cut down or control substance use

5.   a great deal of time is spent in activities necessary to obtain the substance (e.g., visiting multiple doctors or driving long distances), use the substance (e.g., chain-smoking), or recover from its effects

6.   important social, occupational, or recreational activities are given up or reduced because of substance use

7.   the substance use is continued despite knowledge of having a persistent or recurrent physical or psychological problem that is likely to have been caused or exacerbated by the substance (e.g., current cocaine use despite recognition of cocaine-induced depression, or continued drinking despite recognition that an ulcer was made worse by alcohol consumption) (p. 197)

Therapeutic Alliance: The therapeutic alliance involves mutual acceptance of counseling goals and the client-therapist bond. The scientific literature describes the therapeutic alliance by many terms including therapeutic relationship, therapeutic alliance, helping relationship, or working alliance.

Therapist: A therapist in this study is a state certified or licensed counselor trained to provide psychotherapy to a general or specific population.

Therapy Dog: Therapy dogs are usually the personal pets of their handlers, and work with their handlers to provide services to others. They function to enhance the lives of human beings through emotional and physical support. They differ from service dogs, which are trained to do work or perform specific physical tasks for the benefit of an individual with a disability.

Therapy Team: The therapy animal and their handler are a team. For the purposes of this study, the team includes a therapy dog, certified as a Delta Society, Pet-Partner and the handler is a PHD level licensed therapist.

Visiting Program: A visitation program occurs when animals accompany their handlers to a facility and visit with the patients or residents. The main goal of this type of program is socialization and not goal directed therapy such as with AAT.

Assumptions of the Study

The assumptions of this study are as follows:

1. Research participants were able to understand the requirements of the study and the test expectations.

2. Research participants reported their demographic information and perceptions of the group sessions accurately and honestly.

3. Research bias did not skew the results of this study.

4.   The therapist and therapy dog did not have a previous relationship with the clients in this study.

Limitations of the Study

This study was limited to lower income residential treatment clients from South Central Kentucky. While many factors may be applicable to other populations, the clients in this study had many common demographic characteristics specific to this area of the country and to a community care agency dedicated to the treatment for individuals without the abundance of monetary options. Other limitations of the study are as follows:

1. The sample changed over time with clients leaving the groups while other clients joined in the study.

2. The population was homogeneous in both educational levels and in socioeconomic status. Generalization to other populations of clients in residential substance abuse treatment may not be possible.

3. The research participants did not have a previous professional relationship with the researcher, which could have potentially affected the researcher's objectivity. The researcher, as the facility manager, intentionally removed himself from the group therapy process; however, unforeseen conflicts could have existed.

Scope of the Study

This study looked at adult clients in residential substance abuse treatment. The study explored if a relationship exists between AAT and the therapeutic alliance in group treatment. The scope indicates there are commonalities of factors, which can generally apply to other clients in substance abuse treatment. With these commonalities, it is possible to design an effective AAT protocol that will assist substance abuse treatment providers to help clients on their road to recovery. Additionally, the combination of the test instruments, questionnaires and interviews used in this study can provide an effective combination for future research with this and other populations.

Significance of the Study

The implications for social change for the verified hypothesis are profound. First, social change may ensue by influencing treatment programs worldwide by adding a complementary evidence-based practice to addiction treatment providers. Secondly, for those already using AAT in treatment, social change will transpire by verifying empirically what practitioners already suspected anecdotally; specifically, that therapy animals enhance treatment outcome.

Summary

This chapter introduced the study to test the effectiveness of AAT with substance abuse clients in group therapy. The next chapter will explore the literature related to the subject of animal assisted therapy, the therapeutic alliance, and substance abuse treatment. It will conclude with a need for additional empirical research. Details of the methodology of the study are in chapter 3. Test design, instrumentation, data analysis are all defined in chapter 3, along with the research subjects, facility, therapist, and researcher.

CHAPTER 2
REVIEW OF THE LITERATURE

Introduction

This chapter summarizes relevant literature on specific topics related to this research study. Topics reviewed are (a) substance abuse treatment, (b) the therapeutic alliance, (c) animal assisted therapy (AAT), (d) methodology, and (e) theoretical foundations. These topics relate specifically to the research variables in this study. A discussion will follow on the need for empirical research in the investigation of AAT.

Criteria for inclusion in this literature review included identified books, theses and dissertations, and journal articles that contained empirical data or dedicated discussion of issues of relevance to animal assisted therapy, the therapeutic alliance, and substance abuse treatment. This selective review came from thousands of references. The search strategy included keyword searching of online databases from Western Kentucky University, Lindsey Wilson College and Walden University including Medline, PsychInfo, ERIC, Health Source: Nursing/Academic Edition and EBSCO Animals using the terms *animal assisted therapy, animal assisted activities, pet therapy, therapeutic relationship, therapeutic alliance, group therapy*, and *substance abuse treatment*. Most books and journal articles came from the library of Western Kentucky University. Many references came from the university's inter-library loan service. Hand searching of some journals provided many resources, which were not included on the databases. Journals hand-searched included the American Behavioral Scientist and Anthrozoos. First-level cross-reference searches produced articles that were particularly relevant and were not in keyword electronic searches. This also provided the impetus for further hand searching. Leaders of the Delta Society were contacted requesting relevant contributions. No correspondence resulted from this inquiry. A dedicated add-on template package, 'Reference Point Software', with 'Microsoft Word' helped manage the references and produce the citations in the body of the text.

Drug abuse and dependency continues to be a major problem in American society. According to (Bureau of Justice Statistics, 2005a) about a quarter of convicted property and drug offenders committed their crimes to get money for drugs or alcohol. In 2003, there were 5.4 million violent victimizations of United States residents age 12 or older. About 29% of the victims of violence reported that the offender was using drugs or alcohol (Bureau of Justice Statistics, 2005b). According to the last estimation of drug and alcohol's cost to society from 1992, $245.7 billion are lost to society due to the increase in healthcare costs, costs associated with reduced job productivity and other costs such as crime and social welfare (NIDA, 1998). With increased inflation and the new epidemic of methamphetamine abuse, the costs to society have probably increased significantly leaving the social scientists the responsibility to find solutions.

Substance Abuse Treatment

Substance abuse researchers and providers alike have attempted to find the best treatment strategies to work with this unique population. However, these attempts to identify the best treatment strategies and philosophies have resulted in very few answers. Project MATCH (Project Match Research Group, 1997) was an unprecedented research study organized by the National Institute on Alcohol Abuse and Alcoholism to appraise the impact of three different types of treatment (Coping Skills, Motivational Enhancement, and Twelve-Step) for alcohol dependent subjects. The project made special reference to consumer characteristics that might predict better outcomes for each treatment for different types of clients. Treatment was on an outpatient basis for 3 months with outcomes being measured at three-month intervals until a year after treatment, and then measurements were done at 3 years and finally at 10 years (Tonigan et al., 2004). The results of the study indicate that treatment for alcoholism does work but that all treatment modalities work about equally well (Holder et al. 2000).

Rather than describe differences of different theoretical approaches to substance abuse treatment, the focus of this research project will be to embrace the concept of change that is client-directed rather than a theory driven approach. This approach is more concerned with successful outcome instead of competent service delivery outlined by a predefined theoretical model. While theoretical schools continue to espouse their own unique methods, forty years of outcome research has not found any one method to be more reliable than the rest (Duncan & Miller, 2000). In the "Heroic Client", Duncan & Miller advocate for the...

> Removal of theory-directed lenses from our
> professional camera; these lenses can only be focused
> on viewing technique as God and client as Godzilla.
> Instead, we propose to mount a far more powerful
> client-directed lens to view the process of change.
> This lens provides a close-up of the client's
> experiences of therapy, and is focused on client

competencies, perceptions, and ideas (Duncan & Miller, p. 218).

Research demonstrates that the client perceptions of the therapeutic alliance are the most reliable predictor of improvement and positive change (Blatt, Zuroff, Quinlan, & Pilkonis, 1996; Lafferty, Beutler, & Crago, 1989; Gurman, 1977). Bachelor (1991) found that the client's perspective is a much better predictor of outcome than the perspective of the therapist. The fact that clients' ratings of the therapeutic alliance being predictive of positive outcome, should accentuate the necessity for therapists to adhere to a client-centered modality rather than a theory driven approach (Harvath & Symonds, 1991).

The National Institute of Drug Abuse (2000) produced the first science-based guide to the treatment of drug addiction based on a 30-year review of the data. The first of 13 core principles included the principle that "no single treatment works for everyone" pg. 1. It is best when the therapist can bend their theory around the needs of the client rather than the client forced to conform to the boundaries of the therapists' theoretical foundation. Intentional utilization of the client's theory of change by adopting the client's perceptions of the presenting complaint, its causes, and potential solutions facilitates a favorable alliance, increases client participation, and ultimately enhances positive outcome for sobriety (Hubble, Duncan, & Miller, 1999).

The quality of the alliance is an active factor of outcome and not a result of success (Gaston et al., 1991). Hester, Miller, Delaney, and Delaney (1990) compared the effectiveness of traditional 12-step approaches to addiction treatment and a learning based approach. Clients who believed that addiction problems were a disease were much more likely to be sober at the follow-up period if they had received the traditional 12-step addiction treatment. In contrast, clients who believed that addiction problems were a bad habit were more likely to be successful if they had participated in the learning based therapy. It was the client match and not the specific model that made the difference in the clients.

Miller, Taylor, and West (1980) researched the effectiveness of various substance abuse models with the goal of limiting the alcohol consumption for problem drinkers. They also collected data on the contribution of therapist empathy to client outcome. Data revealed that client ratings of therapist empathy correlated significantly with client outcome, accounting for 67% of the variance on the criteria. The results indicate again the importance of therapist empathy and the therapeutic alliance rather than the specific technique or theoretical model used. It is the quality of the alliance that provides the context in which specific techniques exert their influence.

A recent study by Meier, Donmall, McElduff, Barrowclough, and Heller (2006) concluded that addiction professionals attending to the therapeutic alliance in residential drug treatment, influenced retention in therapy. They found that low alliance ratings resulted in higher levels of treatment dropout rates and the client returning to their drug behaviors. When counselors assessed alliance ratings they were able to intervene early and reduce the risk of disengagement from treatment.

Group therapy provides the addict or alcoholic a wide array of persons upon whom they can depend on or direct their deep emotions. By virtue of the number of group members, the group format dilutes the intensity of the feelings, with close interpersonal relationships. While this process is likely to be threatening in a one-to-one environment, the group provides a safer holding environment that gives substance abusers more space, while permitting them to deal with the intense hostility and ambivalence thy are sure to experience as their need for approval, dependence, and caring surface. This is especially true for clients with comorbid psychiatric disorders (Robbins, 2006).

Group therapy is the treatment of choice for substance abuse and addiction (Brook & Spitz, 2002). Group therapy, like attachment theory, is an implied notion that the essence of being human is social, not individual. As previously noted, research findings suggest repeatedly that a positive therapeutic alliance or secure attachment is the best predictor of good outcome in all forms of psychotherapy. The emphasis on the significance of the attachment bond is comparable to the strength of the therapeutic alliance. Nowhere is this more true than with the addicted client, and nowhere is this more difficult to sustain than with the substance-using individual (Flores, 2004).

Developing a therapeutic alliance is a central responsibility of the group therapist. In contrast to individual therapy, this alliance embraces multiple relationships. In group therapy the context is a system of many individuals and relationships rather than the single relationship between two individuals found in individual therapy (Fuhriman & Burlingame, 1990). Burlingame and colleagues (2001) examined the relationship between the therapeutic alliance and successful treatment outcome in group psychotherapy. They indicate that the literature shows cohesion in group as the primary organizational context, within which all successful treatment in group occurs. They present empirical evidence that cohesion in group therapy predicts outcome and that a number of studies have concluded a strong positive relationship exists between cohesion in group and with positive client outcome.

From the perspective of the clients, group therapy relationships include member-to-member, member-to-group, and member-to-leader (Yalom, 2005). In the case of a co-therapist, such as in AAT, there are additional relationships consisting of leader-to-group and leader-to-leader. The therapist must keep his or her focus not only on individual growth of the group member but also on the group as a whole. This process involves encouraging the growth of intrapersonal elements of cohesion such as the individual's sense of belonging and acceptance and a personal allegiance to the group. It also includes intragroup elements such as magnetism and compatibility felt among the group; mutual fondness and trust, support, caring, shared learning, inspiration and a collective dedication to the group work task (Norcross, 2002).

Studies comparing rankings of Yalom's (2005) twelve therapeutic factors reveal that cohesion is the single most important factor in successful treatment especially when conducting groups for substance abusers (Flores 1997). Those findings support Yolom's clinical opinion that the establishment of a cohesive environment is necessary before any other therapeutic forces come out of the group experience. Group cohesion is one of the primary factors necessary for positive therapeutic outcome. Cohesion refers to factors that define the essence of all attachment relationships in group that provide the necessary milieu within which therapy or treatment occurs. Cohesion is to group psychotherapy what the therapeutic alliance is to individual therapy. Just as treatment effectiveness in individual therapy will be limited if a therapeutic alliance is not established, little will be accomplished without cohesion first being developed in group. Group cohesiveness has shown a linear positive relationship with patient improvement in nearly every available report (Tschuschke & Dies, 1994). Empathy, warmth, friendliness, genuineness, and a good therapeutic alliance relate to group cohesion and positive outcome (Marziali, Munroe-Blum, & McCleary, 1997). A minimum level of interaction and self-disclosure is also a major component of high levels of cohesion (Tschuschke & Dies). Additionally, high levels of self-disclosure are correlated with high levels of interpersonal feedback between members, which brings levels of cohesion even higher. As personal detail of disclosure increases the perceived interpersonal distance between members are decreased (Bunch, Lund, & Wiggins, 1983). Unfortunately, the cause and effect relationship in group therapy is not easy to test. Relationships between cohesion and other positive features of group therapy such as self-disclosure, feedback, listening, and empathy often make it difficult to distinguish between cause and effect (Braaten, 1990). Healthy self-disclosure seems to progress overtime from informational matter to more personal information (McKenzie, 1994).

A unique aspect of AAT group therapy is how group members' interactions with the therapy animal might reflect the formation of cohesion and role development among group members. The addition of a therapy animal in a group therapy session requires the group facilitator to be aware of the potential dynamics stimulated by the animal's presence and assimilate this information to understand the group more fully (Chandler, 2005).

Adherence to these client centered principles increases the odds that a client can be successful in individual and group therapy but research and low success rates still indicate a need for innovative treatment techniques for this population. According to Chandler (2005), "Pet practitioners can be especially helpful when working with populations who might be discouraged, unmotivated, resistant, or defiant or who have poor self-insight, deficits in social skills, or barriers to helping relationships" (p 8). Although she never mentions the substance abuse population in her book, she described the addiction population perfectly. Results of this study on AAT could give additional options for substance abuse treatment programs. The next section will focus on the therapeutic alliance, which is the primary element of therapy that produces successful outcomes.

The Therapeutic Alliance

Attachment, alliance, bonding, friendship, mutual physiological regulation, and love are nothing but semantic attempts to define and explain all the intricate subtleties and nuances involved in intimate relationships. The early and simplified concept of the therapeutic alliance was restricted to the positive transference from the patient to the analyst (Freud, 1913). Currently, the therapeutic alliance is viewed as an agreement on the therapeutic tasks and goals, and the development of bonds of mutual trust, acceptance, and confidence between client and therapist (Norcross, 2002). According to attachment theory, both the therapist's and the client's attachment styles contribute to the establishment of the alliance. Each brings something to the therapeutic alliance. It is the strength of the alliance that will repair the empathic collapse that predictably occurs during the course of therapy (Flores, 2004).

The therapist is a central agent of change in the lives of their clients (Crits-Christoph et al., 1991; Lambert & Okiishi, 1997). However, it is not always what a therapist might say to their clients, the theory base or the techniques used, but the behavior and character of the therapist and the alliance created that can make the greatest possible change in the life of the client. Research suggests that preexisting patient characteristics and the therapist education, experience and interventions influences the therapeutic alliance (Crits-Christoph & Connolly Gibbons, 2003).

The "Dodo Bird Effect" is the term attributed to the phenomena that came out of historic outcome research, which found that therapeutic approaches produced similar amounts of outcome gains (Smith & Glass, 1977; Luborsky et al. 2002). Soon afterward researchers began to identify the therapeutic alliance as a major component influencing therapeutic outcomes (Crits-Christoph et al., 1991; Wampold, 2001).

The therapeutic alliance involves mutual acceptance of counseling goals and the client-therapist bond. Counseling relationships are more likely to rely on empathy, rather than authority, to involve the client in treatment (Miller, 1999). Research confirms that the therapeutic alliance accounts for more variance in explaining treatment outcomes than almost all other constructs. The quality of the interaction and client-therapist bond is the factor that constitutes positive outcomes. The therapeutic alliance is a conduit by which techniques and theories must pass before they can achieve their potential. Without a positive alliance it is less likely that the client will accept and adhere to the principles and techniques used by the therapist. As Lambert and Barley (2001) suggest, it is the therapist's ability to relate that creates the capacity for attachment and leads to establishment of a working alliance, without much effort on the client's behalf. The therapist has little opportunity to apply the technical skills that the theory dictates if there is no therapeutic attachment. Creating and maintaining the attachment or therapeutic alliance with alcoholics and addicts requires a special set of skills and knowledge about what constitutes addiction.

In one early meta-analysis by Harvath and Symonds (1991), 24 studies met the narrowed criteria for investigation into the therapeutic alliance. The study concluded that a healthy correlation exists between a healthy therapeutic alliance and positive therapy outcome. Another research project by Martin, Garske, and Davis (2000) used similar criteria as the Harvath and Symonds study looking at an additional 55 studies bringing the research up to date for the time. Their examination continued to identify a large correlation between the therapeutic alliance and measurable outcome. They concluded, as with other studies, that the strength of the therapeutic alliance was predictive of a positive treatment outcome.

A positive therapeutic alliance is one of the best predictors of outcome success. Orlinsky, Ronnestad, and Wilutzki (2003) identified over 1,000 research studies that indicate how positive outcomes depend on an affirmative therapeutic alliance. In many studies, the quality of the alliance and not the technique or theory was predictive of outcome success. According to Wampold (2001) the therapeutic alliance accounted for 54% of the variance of the impact of therapy. A large National Institute of Mental Health (NIMH) study in depression comparing numerous therapies including cognitive behavioral, interpersonal and antidepressant therapists with a placebo found that the therapeutic alliance was predictive of outcome success over the specific therapy used in every research condition (Krupnick et al. 1996).

Clinical training, experience, and research findings accentuate that the therapeutic alliance accounts for as much as, and probably more of, the outcome variance than specific treatments (Orlinsky, Grawe, & Parks, 1994). Techniques account for only 12% to 15% of the variance across the different therapies (Lambert, 1992). Henry (1998) concluded, "The largest chunk of outcome variance not attributable to preexisting patient characteristics involves individual therapist differences and the emergent therapeutic alliance between patient and therapist, regardless of technique or school of therapy. This is the main thrust of three decades of empirical research" (p. 128).

Norcross, (2000), put together a task force on Empirically Supported Therapeutic Alliances of the APA Division of Psychotherapy to extend and compile a finite list of empirically validated interventions. He concluded, as with other studies, that a positive therapeutic alliance has been linked to successful treatment outcome in a myriad of research studies (Martin, Garske, & Davis, 2000; Wampold, 2001). He also believes that therapists need to attend to signs that the therapeutic alliance is working. One way for the therapist to assess the therapeutic alliance is by using objective measures to determine if the alliance is effective.

Assessment tools are best completed by the client. The client is more qualified to provide valid ratings of the therapeutic alliance than the therapist (Bachelor & Horvath, 1999). The most direct impact a therapist can have on outcome change would be to build on the client's perception of the therapeutic alliance (Duncan, Miller, & Sparks, 2004). The therapist must also be aware of their own stress and use their own career sustaining behaviors and coping skills, which are an important variable that relate to more positive therapeutic alliances with clients (Briggs, 2006).

Clients with substance abuse disorders can be a difficult population with which to develop a strong therapeutic alliance. This can be especially true for clients in drug court, on probation or parole and/or other mandated treatment and receiving services in a community mental health agency providing substance abuse treatment to the indigent population. Many clients who are part of, or have been part of, the criminal justice system have a very difficult time trusting professionals, making the working alliance very difficult. Additionally, confrontation and imposing judgment, very common in substance abuse treatment, can create barriers that impair the therapeutic alliance (Miller & Rollnick, 2002).

Individuals with substance abuse and dependency disorders benefit from a good therapeutic alliance. One large study of diverse therapies for alcohol dependency by Connors, DiClemente, Carroll, Longabaugh, and Donovan (1997), indicated that the therapeutic alliance was predictive of recovery success. Just as indicated above, the theoretical models or techniques did not indicate statistical relevance or were predictive of recovery. The therapeutic alliance made the difference. Another study by Chafetz et al. (1962) indicated that in a single empathic counseling session, alcoholics were ten times more likely to seek treatment and almost fifty times as likely to stay in treatment.

A positive, collaborative therapeutic alliance is essential for successful substance abuse treatment (Beck et al. 1993). Therapists need to connect with their clients and gain their trust to develop a positive therapeutic alliance. If a positive therapeutic alliance is not developed, the client will be less likely to benefit from therapy, and could contribute to them dropping out of treatment and relapsing (Meier, Donmall, McElduff, Barrowclough, & Heller, 2006).

The role of a therapist to act as an agent of change in the life of a substance abuse client is more limited and fragile than with other patient populations. A look into the client's family life often reveals that he or she finds more gratification from alcohol and drugs than from the love and support of significant others, friends and relatives (Brennan, Moos, & Kelly, 1994). The positive social reinforcement from a supportive therapist may pale in comparison to the high that the patient gets from their drug of choice. Therefore, it is in the best interest of both the client and therapist to build the alliance when the patient is in a period of diminished drug use or abstinence (Miller & Rollnick, 2002). A strategic approach to the sessions should include underscoring the benefits of having meaningful interpersonal relationships at the same time that the drawbacks of drug use are reinforced. The strategy is to enhance the patient's perceived reasons for remaining drug free, to motivate the patient to strive for relationship preservation, and to communicate the kind of therapeutic support that the patient will value (Miller et al.).

Substance abusers often enter treatment with ambivalence about relinquishing their habits (Carroll et al. 1991a, 1991b; Havassy et al.1991). Within the framework of Prochaska and colleagues' (1993), stages of change model, many substance abusers do not enter treatment at the stages of action or maintenance. Rather, they begin therapy with the notion that it might be beneficial to give up the use of drugs or with an irresolute desire to cut back on their use (i.e., the contemplative stage). However, in cases such as those who are remanded by the courts to attend drug abuse rehabilitation sessions, the patients may not acknowledge a problem with drugs or willing to work toward change (the precontemplative stage).

From the beginning, therapists will need to assess their clients' commitment to change in order to have the best chance of communicating empathy and to minimize the risk of pushing an unwanted agenda and increasing resistance onto their clients. It is good to keep in mind that to accuse patients of "not really wanting to change", or of "wanting to suffer", or of "being in denial" can be detrimental (Miller et al., 2002) especially in an outpatient setting. In this setting, the patient can easily leave treatment and never return if he or she takes offense at the therapist's methods. It would be much better to acknowledge that the patient has mixed emotions and then to assess and get to know the one side of the client who likes to use drugs and the other side would rather be free of them. In this manner, the therapist demonstrates that he or she is not so naïve as to believe that the client's goal is absolute and immediate abstinence, but rather recognizes the complexities and difficulties involved in trying to stop using drugs. Additionally, the therapist avoids the potentially damaging snare of communicating in a judgmental, unempathic manner, which would harm the alliance (Miller et al.).

Animal Assisted Therapy (AAT)

Introduction and Definitions

AAT is defined by the Delta Society (2004) as "a goal-directed intervention in which an animal that meets specific criteria is an integral part of the treatment process." AAT or animal assisted activities (AAA) is used in a variety of programs to increase an individual's physical, social, emotional, and cognitive functioning. Therapeutic animals can function as a companion, social facilitator (Hunt, Hart, & Gomulkiewicz, 1992) and as a therapeutic co-facilitator.

AAT is an adjunct to existing therapy. A therapist can incorporate the animal into whatever professional style or theoretical approach the therapist already enacts. AAT can be directive or nondirective in its approach. Individual or group therapy can integrate AAT sessions for use with a wide variety of populations. Chandler (2005) offers several suggestions why therapy pets can alter the dynamics of the therapy process. They are as follows:

1. The client may be more motivated to attend and participate in therapy because of a desire to spend time with the therapy pet.
2. The client's focus shifts away from disabling pain because of the interaction with the therapy pet to the extent that the client can work harder and longer in therapy and potentially gain more benefits per session.
3. The client may receive healing nurturance and affection through physical contact with the therapy pet.
4. The client may experience soothing comfort from petting or holding the therapy pet.
5. The client may experience unconditional acceptance by the therapy pet.
6. The client may experience enjoyment and entertainment from interactions with the therapy pet.
7. The client may be able to form a more trusting relationship with the therapist who demonstrates he or she can be trusted by the way the therapist interacts with the therapy animal.
8. In many instances, based on the unique characteristic of the client's condition or needs, the client may be able to perform activities and achieve goals that would not otherwise be possible without the assistance of a therapy pet. (Chandler, 2005, pp. 3-4).

AAT is an adjunct tool used by therapists during typical individual or group counseling sessions. A nondirective therapist may simply introduce the therapy animal to the clients and explain that petting or playing with the pet during a session is a standing invitation during any point of the client's session. A directive therapist usually structures interventions for the client aided by interaction with the pet, all done with the permission of the client. These sessions also include an invitation for the client to interact with the pet during the session by petting or holding it (Delta Society, 1996).

The therapist may pet the therapy animal that seeks affection from the therapist during the therapy session. This nurturing interaction provides useful information to the client about the positive and trusting alliance between the therapist and the pet and may help the client feel more comfortable with the therapist after observing such gentle behavior. Both the therapist and the client petting and interacting with the animal take the therapeutic alliance even to another level of trust (Delta Society, 1996).

To understand the usage of animal assisted therapy, it is important to first to look at the historical context. The next section will examine the history of AAT.

Historical Context

Domesticated animals have played a significant role in the lives of humans for thousands of years. In the 9th century, during the early middle ages, the people of Gheel, Belgium provided care for the disabled in which animals played an essential therapeutic role (Catanzaro, 2003). The first documented modern use of animals in treatment was in 1792 by the York Retreat for the mentally disturbed (Tuke, 1964). Rather than using the familiar cruel treatment methodologies of the time, the Quakers introduced animals to their asylum programming. This animal treatment helped patients become more externally oriented and reality-based (McCulloch, 1986).

A treatment home in Bethel, Germany also introduced animals to their patients in 1867. The home allowed the patients to interact with and care for various animals including birds, dogs, cats, horses and other farm animals. The animals affected the patients positively but no recorded observations survive (Netting, Wilson, &

New, 1987). Even the famous nurse, Florence Nightingale, recognized the benefits of animal interaction. She wrote about her pet owl, Athena, whom she loved in life and mourned in death. Athena was stuffed and currently displayed at Nightingale's childhood home. She once wrote, "A pet bird in a cage is sometimes the only pleasure of an invalid confined for years to the same room" (Nightingale, 1860, p. 58).

AAT was first documented in the United States in 1919 when Franklin Lane, the Secretary of the Interior advised using dogs with psychiatric patients at St. Elizabeth's Hospital in Washington, DC (Hooker, Freeman, & Stewart, 2002). Another early use of animals used in therapy in the United States was at Pawling Air Force Convalescent Hospital in Pawling, New York. Various animals were used in World War II to motivate the servicemen to participate in therapy and provide friendship as they recuperated from both physical and emotional trauma (Davis, 1988). In 1944 Bossard wrote about the benefits of animals with humans. He noted how important pet animals are to the wellbeing of the family and overall mental health of the children. He referenced how dogs can be a source of unconditional love and an object for family members to express love and affection and teach responsibility (Bossard, 1944).

Boris Levinson was the first to document the benefits of and coin the term *pet therapy*. In the 1960s, he inadvertently allowed his dog "Jingles" into therapy sessions and observed dramatic improvement with resistant clients (Levinson, 1966). He continued as a pioneer of AAT and wrote of his accounts with his dog (Levinson, 1969, 1972). Yet, despite his research and experience, his professional colleagues met Boris Levinson with ridicule and scorn when he gave a presentation of his observations of AAT at the annual meeting of the American Psychological Association. One scoffer even asked the doctor if his dog shared his therapy fees (Levinson, 1984).

In the 1970s and 1980s, use and research on AAT and AAA began to flourish. Friedmann, Katcher, Lynch, and Thomas (1980) published the first study in a medical journal that documented animal ownership as a factor that contributed to the prevention of disease. They found that pet owners had increased health benefits after discharge from a coronary care unit as compared to non-pet owners. In 1988 the National Institute of Health (NIH) convened the NIH Technology Assessment Workshop on the health benefits of pets (National Institutes of Health, 1988). Hines (2003) outlined the first national and international organizations and centers devoted to AAT and AAA. They are listed in order of their founding.

1974	Joint Advisory Committee on Pets in Society (United Kingdom)
1976	Association Francaise d'Information et de Recherche sur l'Animal de Compagnie (France)
1977	Institute for Interdisciplinary Research on the Human-Pet Relationship (Austria)
1977	Center on Interaction of Animals and Society
1977	Delta Foundation that in 1981 became Delta Society
1979	Group for the Study of Human-Companion Animal Bond that in 1982 became Society for Companion Animal Studies (United Kingdom)
1980	Joint Advisory Committee on Pets in society (Australia)
1981	AVMA Task Force on the Human-Animal Bond
1981	Animal Medical Center Institute for the Human-Companion Animal Bond
1981	Center to Study Human-Animal Relationships and Environments

1982   Center for Applied Ethnology and Human-Animal
              Interactions, (In 1997 it became the Center for the
              Human-Animal Bond)

Specific Populations.

According to Folse, Minder, Aycock, and Santana (1994), AAT has enhanced the lives of various populations including inpatient psychiatric patients, patients with cancer, heart disease, AIDS or Alzheimer's disease, children with emotional disorders and disabilities and survivors of sexual abuse. AAT is utilized in individual, family and group therapy sessions with a diverse population and across the life span of the clients (Fine, 2000, 2006). Counselors are seeing the most dramatic positive effects of working with a therapy animal with the dysfunctional or highly resistant clients as compared to the same work without a therapy animal (Chandler, 2005).

This researcher has focused his efforts on some of the best empirically based research on AAT. However, many of the following studies for AAT did not introduce animals as a goal-directed intervention but simply as a part of a pet visitation program. Although such programs may produce desirable effects in these special populations, AAT is unique by incorporating specific goals into treatment under the guidance of a professional therapist.

Anxiety, stress and physical health. Animals are included in family television shows, commercials, and advertisements to make the setting less threatening and more homelike to their viewers. Clients perceive images with an individual and their pet as happier, friendlier, and more relaxed than images with people without a pet (Paul, 2000). In a therapeutic environment a therapy animal has the capacity to enhance the therapeutic climate by helping reduce stress, calm the client and lower blood pressure and heart rates.

Calming effects with AAT and AAA have been found among various therapeutic settings and various populations such as children with posttraumatic stress disorder (Altschuler, 1999), attention deficit hyperactivity disorder, conduct disorders and even Down's syndrome (Hart, 2000). Animals can be a stress reducer by giving tactile comfort and offering recreational distraction from daily worries (Hart, 2000). These studies demonstrate the relationship between tactile comfort and recreational distraction on reducing stress in individuals with the above disorders.

Companion animals can serve as a buffer against anxiety producing situations and influence conditions that decrease the onset, severity and progression of stress-related conditions (Wilson, 1991). In perceived threatening situations, people feel safer in the presence of a friendly animal regardless if the perceived threat is real. Pets have a way of normalizing stressful situations (Hart, 2000). According to Cusack (1988) animals can help take a person's mind off their fears, being great distracters during or outside of therapy. Physiological indicators of stress and anxiety such as heart rate and blood pressure decrease when a therapy animal is present (Baun, Bergastrom, Langston, & Thoma, 1984; Nagengast, Baun, Megel, & Leibowitz, 1997). According to one study by Odendaal, (2000), six neurochemicals associated with a decrease in blood pressure were positively associated with animal interaction.

In a study by Barker and Dawson (1998) AAT helped lower anxiety levels among various hospitalized psychiatric patients. The populations tested were patients classified as having mood disorders, psychotic disorders, substance use disorders and "all other disorders" which included individuals with anxiety, personality, and cognitive disorders. The results of the study indicated a decrease in anxiety levels for every group except for the substance use group. It is unsure why the substance use group did not have the same results as the other psychiatric populations.

The physical and emotional benefits of AAT, AAA and animal ownerships continue in the research. Pets can reduce the response to stressors and lower ambient blood pressure in mild hypertension (Allen, Blascovich, Tomaka, & Kelsey, 2001; Allen, Shykoff, & Izzo, 2001). Anderson, Reid, and Jennings (1992) reported that pet owners had lower systolic blood pressures, plasma cholesterol, and triglycerides values than non-pet owners. There is a link between a positive neuroendocrine effect with human-animal interaction, including dopamine, cortisol, oxytocin, prolactin, endorphin, and phenylethylamine levels in both the humans and their pet dogs (Odendaal, 1999).

Dog ownership, lower anxiety, and human social support are all associated with an increased likelihood of one-year survival after a myocardial infarction (Friedmann & Thomas, 1995). Pet ownership's influence on psychosocial risk factors seems to be a primary factor in the reduction of cardiovascular disease (Patronek & Glickman, 1993). Pets motivate people to exercise, fight depression, reduce blood pressure, and help prevent heart disease.

AAT is classified as a complementary and alternative medicine (CAM) technique for cancer patients (Johnson, Meadows, Haubner, & Sevedge, 2003). Human-animal interaction has demonstrated beneficial effects on anxiety and despair among cancer patients (Muschel, 1984). When fighting cancer, the patient first needs to fight the debilitating fear and loneliness of the diagnosis. A therapy dog can detect emotional and behavioral changes in their clients. They help make the atmosphere safe for emotions and add a spiritual element to the healing. Whatever the patient is feeling, they can express it to a therapy dog. Patients do not need to feel censored and can freely express themselves without the fear of judgment.

Even well-meaning friends and family will frequently touch a cancer patient cautiously as if they are afraid the cancer was infectious. This turning away from touch, which the client craves so much, can deeply hurt them emotionally and physically (Post-White et al. 2003). Therapy animals love to touch and be touched (Becker, 2002). Hospice patients can particularly benefit from AAT (Chinner & Dalziel, 1991). Finally, pet ownership has helped in depressive symptoms among AIDS patients (Siegel, Angulo, Detels, Wesch, & Mullen, 1999).

Elderly. Older adults can greatly benefit from AAA or AAT. As the population grows older and the baby boom generation moves toward retirement, therapists will need to explore evidence-based therapies to use with these populations. According to Harris, Rinehart, and Gerstman's research (1993), about one third of the elderly population lives alone and could benefit from AAT.

AAT is not a single treatment or technique for the elderly (Cusack, 1988). Instead, the field of AAT falls into three classes: milieu therapy, physical rehabilitation, and pet-facilitated psychotherapy, (Brickel, 1986). In milieu therapy the client and animal coexist in the same environment. With physical rehabilitation, the clients work with the animal such as walking the dog, grooming the animal, or feeding the animal. Pet-facilitated psychotherapy involves the animal helping to link the therapist or therapist's activities with the client by drawing them out verbally or emotionally and providing tactile touch and emotional comfort.

Mosher-Ashley and Barrett (1997) expanded the ideas of Brickel and proposed five forms of AAT for the elderly: functional, relationship, passive, cognitive, and spiritual. The functional form of AAT includes the client caring for the animal, which can bring physical and emotional benefits for the client such as in increased levels of self-esteem, self-confidence, and mobility. The relationship form of AAT is affective in nature, resulting in sensory stimulation and expressions of affection. Passive AAT involves relaxation and stress reduction because of the animal's capacity to entertain their human companions. Pets bring stimulation and enjoyment as well as facilitating increased social interaction between other clients. AAT helps stimulate and expand the cognitive knowledge of the caregiver. For example, in equine therapy the client will learn all parts of the animal and tack. The spiritual form of AAT includes stimulating memories of pleasurable experiences with animals from the past. It involves the client developing a sense of oneness with life and God's creation.

AAT is in nursing homes and adult visiting services to improve social interaction, psychosocial function, life satisfaction, social competence, and psychological well-being, all the while reducing depression and loneliness, hopelessness and social withdrawal. Playful animals can play a positive role for elderly persons in need of stimulation and the need to care for another (Siegel, 1990, 1993). Pet owners have raised levels of life satisfaction and personal safety when compared with non-owners (Norris, Shinew, Chick, & Beck, 1999).

One of the earliest experimental studies on AAT was done with elderly subjects in England (Mugford & McComisky, 1975). In a study by Corson and Corson (1978), researchers gave puppies or adult dogs to geriatric patients to care for and train. The results clearly showed that the patients had an increase in physical activity and social interactions.

The documented physiological and psychological benefits of animal interaction for the elderly served as the catalyst for animal visits to become common practice in retirement centers and nursing homes throughout America (Arkrow, 1993). Nursing homes and other older adult residential programs use AAA or AAT in a variety of ways from having an animal resident mascot to allowing for visiting animals. Older adults with Alzheimer's disease can benefit from almost every kind of animal contact (Verderber, 1991). Alzheimer's patients can benefit from AAT by increasing social behaviors such as smiles, laughs, looks, and tactile response (Batson,

McCabe, Baun, & Wilson, 1997). Therapy dogs can help provide a focal point and motivation as well as organize their thinking. Fish tanks improve eating habits and increase eye coordination (Edwards & Beck, 2002).

Providing care for a pet can serve as a buffer against loneliness and isolation and bring increased levels of activity with the aged. Isolation can lead to depression, and depression can lead to elevated stress, which in turn can make an individual susceptible to various diseases. Depression and stress can raise the odds of dying. According to Taylor, Maser, Yee, and Gonzalez (1993), the elderly have had positive results from AAT such as smiling, laughing, alertness, motivation, socialization, physical activity, and self-esteem. One study by Churchill, Safaoui, McCabe, and Baun (1999) indicated the presence of a therapy dog helped increase socialization among clients with Alzheimer's disease. This group of clients demonstrated increases in verbalizations, smiles, looks, leans, and tactile contact. The clients also demonstrated lower levels of aggressive behaviors especially in the evening hours when increased levels of restlessness, cognitive confusion, paranoia, and aimless wandering were common.

In a related study, researchers introduced male nursing home clients a therapy dog in a socialization group. The results of the study showed that twice the interaction occurred in the AAT group showing that the presence of the dog provided a comfortable environment for facilitating interpersonal communication skills among nursing home elderly clients (Fick, 1993).

A decrease in noise levels, including loud spontaneous vocalizations and aggressive verbal outbursts were another benefit of AAT with elderly psychiatric patients (Walsh, Mertin, Verlander, & Pollard, 1995). In this study, the nursing staff also observed an increase in pro-social interactions between the psychiatric patients and other patients or staff by the group exposed to the dog. Research by Barak, Savorai, Mavashev, and Beni (2001) show how AAT may be an excellent treatment option to promote quality of life and reduce stress in institutionalized patients. Francis (1976) found that among 500 individuals who were in long-term care facilities, the most frequently missed thing was a pet animal. These results indicate that a therapy dog can improve the social climate of an institution, which could include a residential substance abuse treatment center, which is included in this study.

Harris, Rinehart, and Gerstman (1993) studied the effect animals had on the blood pressure of elderly homebound patients. Each elderly participant had to be at least 60 years of age and have a history of pet ownership, but presently have no dog in his or her home. A registered nurse, a volunteer, and a therapy dog visited the patients all within a 4-week period. Assessment for vital signs took place at the beginning and at the end of the visits. The results of the study indicated that the visit with just a nurse or volunteer did not significantly change the client's blood pressure; however, when the dog joined the visitation team, blood pressure did go down.

Developmentally disabled and the mentally ill. Psychiatric patients are at the forefront of AAT research (Hooker, Freeman, & Stewart, 2002). Dealing with the stigma of admission to a psychiatric inpatient setting lessoned at the presence of and interaction with a dog. For inpatient adolescents, the presence of a dog on the psychiatric unit improved outcomes by redefining the residential milieu and providing unconditional acceptance (Bardill & Hutchinson, 1997). In a recent doctorial research study by Pence (2005), AAT was used with an institutionalized patient suffering from traumatic brain injury and co-morbid depression. The results of the study clearly indicated a decrease in anxiety and increase in social interactions.

Children and adults with physical or emotional handicaps or developmental disabilities have shown that interaction with dogs, horses and even dolphins can be used as a powerful motivator to learn and develop new skills and interact with the world around them (Nathanson, 1998). Marine animals help facilitate therapeutic goals with the developmental disabled population. In a study by Nathanson & de Faria (1994), children with mental retardation showed significant cognitive improvement when working with dolphins when compared with those who did not use this form of therapy. The frequency of verbal responses increased and frequency of no responses decreased when dolphins became reinforcers instead of toys. In an earlier study by Nathanson (1989), dolphins helped increase attention and language skills for children with mental disabilities than were land-based procedures.

Children and youth. Boris Levinson, the founder of AAT, was a child psychologist and paved the way for future research and therapists to add animals to the therapy team for children (Levinson, 1969; 1978; 1984). Unfortunately, the findings of Levinson and a majority of researchers testing the benefits of AAT for children have been anecdotal in nature (Condoret, 1983; Kidd & Kidd, 1986; Reichert, 1998). These early studies demonstrate observable accounts of the therapeutic benefits of AAT but without empirical support. In recent years, empirical research has been clearly demonstrating the benefits of AAT for children.

Most children in America obtain some type of pet during their childhood with currently 63% of American households owning a pet equating to 69 million households (APPMA, 2005). Many individuals can remember their first pet. Animals and children are often displayed together in popular children's books, classic literature, cartoons, and popular movies. Animals can enhance a child's life by bringing comfort, safety, attachment, and love. Animals can further help a child with developmental learning experiences by offering sensorimotor exercise and by being teaching examples for lessons in life and death, grief, sexuality and elimination (Robin & ten Bensel, 1985). Animals attract and draw infants. They are alive and can provide greater stimulation and therapeutic opportunities than toys (Ross, 1983).

Many of today's children live in a time of emotional turmoil. Children will look to their pets for emotional support. According to several studies, many children will turn to their pets when they feel sad, angry, and happy or want to share a secret (Covert, Whirren, Keith, & Nelson, 1985; Melson, 2003). Children who have a strong bond with their pet demonstrate greater empathy toward others (Poresky, 1990). "Latch-key" or "self-care" children who come home from school do not come to an empty home when a pet happily greets them (Heath & McKenry, 1989). Pets will always listen to children and will always have time to play.

Children are the recipients of care and protection but seldom do they have a chance to provide it, unless they have a pet for which they are responsible, putting the animal's needs before their own. Many children learn to nurture by caring for their pets (Melson, 2001). Some studies show that children attached to their pets expressed greater empathy toward their peers (Ascione, 1992; Melson, Peet, & Sparks, 1992). Children increased their empathic response toward other humans when exposed to humane animal education (Ascione, 1992).

The child sees the dog or other therapy animal as accepting and dependent, unlike the adult human therapist who is often seen as an authority figure. The therapy animal can serve as a mediator between the therapist and child. When this happens, the child is usually more receptive to the direction of the therapist (Mallon, 1992).

AAT has contributed to therapy with sexually abused girls. In a study by Reichert (1994), sexually abused girls had the option of disclosing their abuse into a dog's ears as opposed to just telling other group members. The children held the dog before, during, and after the disclosure for extra support. This helped the children disclose more easily and talk about their family histories with lessened anxiety.

The presence of animals reduces stress during medical exams in children. In one study, children who had a medical exam in the presence of a dog had significantly reduced blood pressure, heart rate, and behavioral distress than children who did not have a dog present during the exam (Nagengast, Baun, Leibowitz, & Megel, 1993). Another study by Woolverton (1993) also showed that children were significantly calmed with an animal present, with the animal providing a strong diversion during a neuromuscular examination.

Children with Autistic disorder decrease self-absorption and increase pro-social behaviors with the introduction of a therapy dog (Redefer & Goodman, 1989). Another study by Law and Scott (1995) showed that autistic children increased their socialization with other students, increased their cooperative interactions and discussion and problem solving improved with the introduction of a domestic animal into the classroom. Campbell and Katcher (1992) also found that AAT with a dog resulted in increased social responses to the dog and therapist, and increased attention span and gains in verbal ability among children with autism. Many of the children in the study learned new words and demonstrated much higher interaction rates with either the animal or handler.

Children with Attention Deficit Hyperactivity Disorder (ADHD) have also benefited from AAT. Katcher & Wilkins (1994) demonstrated that AAT significantly improved the residential treatment of boys between the ages of nine and fifteen, many diagnosed with ADHD. In this study, the animal increased the social attractiveness of the therapist, which allowed the children to feel safer when interacting with the therapist. Additionally, the animal helped decrease the agitation and lowered aggressive behavior while improving the cooperation with staff members in a residential community.

Inmates. According to Allen (1989), there are three primary objectives for a prison. First, to have prisoners listen and obey authority; second, to instill a work ethic and third to enhance the morale of the prison staff. Taking the focus off punishment and working toward rehabilitation must be achieved if inmates are to be reintroduced into society and become respectable citizens as well as reduce the financial burden to the community (Strimple, 2003). Introducing animals to felons have shown promise in achieving the goal of rehabilitation, lowering the cost of incarceration, as well as reducing violent acts among the inmates.

A recent novel by Steven King turned Hollywood blockbuster starring Tom Hanks, *The Green Mile* (Darabont, 1999), demonstrated the effect an animal can have on inmates and guards alike. In the film, a smart prison mouse named Mr. Jingles helped calm hardened criminals, brought laughter to death row and helped antisocial men act unselfishly toward others. Another movie and book of the same title that speaks of the therapeutic value of animals was the *Birdman of Alcatraz* (Frankenheimer, 1962). In the movie, starring Burt Lancaster, birds were used therapeutically in one of the toughest prisons in U.S. history. Although the movie was fiction, the birdman of Alcatraz was a real figure, Robert Stroud, who wrote a 500-page book entitled *Digest of Bird Diseases* (Stroud, 1964) before he was incarcerated (Strimple, 2003).

One of the original proponents of AAT in prisons was a psychiatric social worker by the name of David Lee from Lima State Hospital for the criminally Insane in Lima, Ohio. Lee helped develop several AAT programs in this and other correctional facilities. The AAT programs were built around a behavior management system in which the inmate could earn time with the animal and could even earn a mascot to have as their own. The results of the study indicated that when pets were kept, a significant reduction in suicide attempts and violent incidents occurred (Lee, 1983). Other research studies have confirmed similar findings (Corson & Corson, 1978).

In a study by Walsh and Mertin (1996), the responsibility of the care and training of dogs accounted for a statistically significant increase in self-esteem and decrease in depression for women inmates. The women became calmer, less aggressive, and happier while participating in the program. Similar programs for juvenile offenders have also been successful. Project POOCH was a program first developed by the Oregon Department of Education and the Oregon Youth Authority. The purpose was to bring incarcerated youth together with abandoned and abused dogs. The inmates learned by running a boarding kennel where the animals would receive training and proper care. The findings of one study by Merriam-Arduini (2000) resulted in zero recidivism among POOCH participants. The youth changed by showing growth in honesty, empathy, nurturing, social growth, understanding of others, confidence level and pride of accomplishment.

Substance abuse. Two studies address the effects of AAT on substance abuse treatment. The first study was a thesis project on the impact of AAT with an adolescent substance abuse population by Pace (1996). This was a descriptive study, which explored both the impact of AAT on three female adolescents in treatment for substance abuse and the adolescents' role changes and changes in self-concept after AAT. The results of the study found that after AAT the adolescent participants felt an increase in self-concept and patience. The female participants made changes in the roles they plan to assume in the future.

Campbell-Berg (2000) did the second study. The researcher conducted a qualitative study in a 21-day residential treatment program for substance abuse disorders. She took six to eight individuals from the population and conducted four group sessions. In attendance was a German shepherd dog that was free to approach any group member with his toy in anticipation of a game of fetch. The researcher asked a series of 15 questions to the group and the answers formed the data analyzed by the researcher.

The results of the study found that the presence of the dog altered barriers to communication between the group facilitator and the group participants, resulting in enhanced transactions. According to the researchers, the dog's presence helped improve communication, which made the participants have a greater understanding of their personal situation. "Therefore, the individuals were able to gather insight and learned to understand their chemically dependent thinking, manage their feelings and emotions, and interrupt self-defeating drug-seeking behaviors without mood altering drugs"(Campbell-Berg, 2000, p. 33). The study further indicated an increase in positive attitude and hopefulness, trust, communication and reduction in fear and anxiety among the participants.

This study was entirely based on observation of the therapist/researcher. There were no controls or instrumentation used to measure any significance. Although this study was foundational for attempting to use AAT with the substance abuse population, it was poorly constructed and no empirical evidence for AAT with a substance abuse population can be drawn from the results of the study.

Although there is lack of empirical evidence to support AAT directly with the substance abuse population, several programs provide such therapeutic services. AAT, integrated with solution-focused therapy, has also been used in the treatment of one substance abuse counseling program from Colorado (Pichot & Coulter, 2006). This program has proven effective in helping clients recover from alcohol and drug problems. This program helps change the power differential between the professionals and the clients. When a therapist has an animal co-therapist, the professional is often seen as more "human" and approachable. AAT increases the general comfort level of clients in therapy and helps them focus on positive activity instead of the drug culture "war stories". AAT in this program also helps the clients to focus their attention on an external source, which assists with lower anxiety and depression.

Risks

There are a few negatives of AAT and AAA including costs, dislike of animals, phobias and cultural inhibitions (Brodie, Biley, and Shewring, 2002). According to some research studies, pets have no effect on decreased health and morale in some populations (Miller & Lago, 1990; Stallones, Marx, Garrity, & Johnson, 1990). There could be many reasons for this phenomena but Simon (1984) believes that some people have an impaired capacity of intimacy and having a close attachment to a pet can harm the bonds with people. For a limited few, AAT or AAA jeopardizes patients' health. Risks of AAT include the potential of pet death, unpredictable animal actions such as bites, allergens, and zoonoses that can affect the client's health (Chandler, 2005).

Zoonoses are diseases and infections that transmit from the animal to the human. Approximately 35 zootomic diseases can be transmitted in AAT or AAA (Schantz, 1990). Zoonoses can be transmitted to humans in a number of ways including direct contact and being airborne. Fortunately, zoonoses are rare and can be limited with proper veterinary care. Everyone is at risk; however, children, the elderly, and those with immune deficiency diseases are most at risk. Small children are especially susceptible because they can have a more intimate relationship with pets and indulge in behaviors such as pica.

Allergies are another potential hazard of AAA or AAT (Barba, 1995). Animal dander, saliva, hair, urine, and other secretions from animals can all become an allergen for predisposed individuals. An individual handler or program can reduce the risk of allergies to patients by careful selection of the animal. Cats, guinea pigs, and horses are especially bothersome for producing allergens (Schantz, 1990).

Finally, bites from animals are the most serious health related problem for AAT and AAA (Schantz, 1990). It is important that the most troublesome breeds be eliminated as therapy dogs. This supports the need for the animal to have a good temperament, extensive training, and to obtain and maintain certification with a respectable organization.

The benefits of AAT or AAA far outweigh the risks (Marcus & Marcus, 1998). The potential risks to AAT or AAA clients are real; however minimized by simple actions, including careful selection of the animal and client, thorough planning and allocation and responsible, rigorous veterinary care of the animal and informed consent for all involved. Every AAT provider should understand their responsibility for the care of their animal and provide a good diet and quality rest from participation in therapy. The handler must be able to identify stress in the animal and intervene with respite.

Methodology

Just as much of the material on mental health disorders are sponsored by large pharmaceutical companies, so many pet food manufacturers and veterinarian organizations financially support much of the material espousing the benefits of AAT and AAA with little or no empirical support (Brasic, 1998). The conclusions and motivation behind AAT and AAA research need to be assessed with caution. In recent years, there has been a definite increase of empirically supported research in AAT. However, the need for quantitative and superior qualitative research for AAT with the substance abuse population continues.

This quantitative research study included an experimental design using randomized populations and controlled conditions to establish the effects of chosen variables that influence an outcome. It is the desire of this researcher to contribute in a meaningful way to the scientific literature rather than adding another research project with limited or poor data (Barba, 1998; Garrity & Stallones, 1998; Gerbasi, 2004). This would support the scientific community that is calling for better research (Johnson et al, 2002 & Odendaal, 2002).

Theoretical Foundations

Theory helps to lay the foundation for good empirical research. However, according to a study by Gerbasi (2004), a majority of AAT research abstracts do not provide a theoretical explanation of AAT. In her analysis, only 4 of the 128 articles of AAT clearly specified a theoretical explanation of the AAT phenomenon. One reason for this is the lack of consensus on theory for AAT. Kruger and Serpell (2006, pp. 25-26) states, "The field of animal assistedinterventions currently lacks a unified widely accepted, or empirically supported theoretical framework for explaining how and why relationships between humans and animals are potentially therapeutic."

As discussed in chapter one, social support theory is the theory of choice to explain the human benefits of AAT. Social support theory is a multifaceted concept that is widely studied but rarely do theoreticians and research agree on a working definition (Hupcey, 1998). Vaux (1988) believed three constructs accounted for social support: support networks, supportive behaviors, and a subjective appraisal of support. Cohen (1992) was supportive of Vaux's comments, believing that a comprehensive definition should not be used and suggested three aspects of social support: social networks, perceived support, and supportive behaviors. Hupcey (1998) attempted to consolidate many of these concepts and developed five categories of the social support construct; they include: (a) the type of support being provided; (b) the recipients' perception of the support; (c) the intentions or behaviors of the provider; (d) reciprocal support; and (e) social networks.

Numerous authors and theorists (Antonucci & Jackson, 1990; Cobb, 1976; Cohen et al., 1985; Jacobson, 1986; Lin, 1986; Pilisuk, 1982) describe the first category "type" of support by Hupcey (1998). Cobb defines social support as information that leads an individual to believe that he or she is cared for and loved, esteemed and valued, and that he or she belongs to a network of communication and mutual obligation. Cohen et al. (p. 75) describes social support as "the resources that are provided by other persons [or animals]". The second category of social support involves the recipients' perceptions (Albrecht & Adelman, 1987; Heller et al., 1986; Procidano & Heller, 1983; Tilden et al., 1990). According to Procidano and Heller (p. 2) social support is the "extent to which an individual believes that his/her needs for support, information, and feedback are fulfilled". The third category involves the intentions or behaviors of the provider of support (Thoits, 1985; Shumaker & Brownell, 1984). Shumaker and Brownell (1984, p. 13) concluded, "Social support is an exchange of resources between two individuals received by the provider or the recipient to be intended to enhance the well-being of the recipient." With AAT research, the perception of the provider animal is not a consideration. Reciprocity (Vaux, 1992; Antonucci, 1985; Shumaker & Brownell, 1984) defines the fourth category proposed by Hupcey (1998). Antonucci (1985, p. 25) wrote, "The actual giving, receiving and exchange of support is commonly referred to as the function of social support". The final category involves social networks (Young, 2004; Thoits, 1982; Lin et al., 1979; Weiss, 1974). "Social support may be defined as support accessible to an individual through social ties to other individuals, groups, and the larger community" (Lin et al., 1979, p. 109).

Although social support theory was originally theorized with human support in mind it has been easily transferred as a theoretical foundation to explain the physiological and psychological benefits humans experience when around animals. Animals are demonstrably a source of social support as indicated by the number of Americans who say that their pet is a "member of the family" and talk to their pet animal as if it was a human companion or confidant (Beck & Katcher, 2003; Cain, 1983). Although the comment: "member of the family" can mean different things for different individuals (Cohen, 2002), pets can also increase and facilitate human social support (Eddy, Hart, & Boltz, 1988). Animal companions often serve as confidants when people feel alienated or afraid of contact with other humans (Beck & Katcher, 1996). Fick (1993) reported that the presence of animals in nursing homes increase both social and verbal interactions with other humans. The presence of a therapy dog increased verbal and nonverbal interactions with other humans twofold when compared with residents without the dog present.

One facet of animal-to-human social support that differs from human-to-human social support is the perception of the recipient. Unfortunately, many humans will provide social support emerging from social obligation, job duties, or other intentions that could limit the meaning and benefits to the recipient. For example, an individual may provide social support by taking an individual to the store but could complain about this obligation the entire way, making the recipient feel worse than if the event ever happened in the first place. Jung (1988, p. 239) stated that "providers do not appear to bestow support simply because there is a need, but rather they weigh several factors, including appraisal of the potential recipient's responsibility and effort as well as the costs involved for the providers". This is not true for animal providers of social support. Most people do not believe their pets to be selfish or having the complex psychological constructs to be selfish or provide support grudgingly.

Another theory used to explain the effects of AAT is social facilitation theory. This theory does not explain an increase in socialization or other social effects; but instead, social facilitation theory refers to how the presence of others is arousing due to evaluation apprehension and/or competition. This theory explains how performance of a simple or well-learned task will be enhanced in the presence of an audience or how performance of a difficult, complex, or poorly learned task will be impeded by an audience. One study by Zajonc, Heingartner, and Herman (1969) got cockroaches to run down a clear tube towards a light. They ran faster when watched by other cockroaches. When put in a simple maze, it took them longer when they were being watched. Another study by Michaels (1982) and three colleagues overtly watched students play pool. The better players got better. The novices got worse.

The Yerkes-Dodson Law of arousal enhances social facilitation theory for AAT. This law predicts an inverted U-shaped function between arousal and performance (Yerkes & Dodson, 1908). A certain amount of arousal can be a motivator toward learning new behaviors. Too much or too little change will certainly work against the learner. Therapists want some mid-level of arousal for their clients to provide the motivation to change. Too little arousal has an inert effect on the learner, while too much has a hyperactive effect (Gerbasi, 2004). The optimal level of arousal is lower for more difficult or intellectually challenging tasks because the clients need to concentrate on the material and higher for tasks requiring endurance and persistence because the clients need more motivation. Well-learned or frequently practiced tasks perform best at higher levels of arousal, whereas poorly learned, difficult and/or infrequently practiced tasks perform best at lower levels of arousal.

With Yerkes-Dodson Law and social facilitation theory, the presence of the therapist while part of the treatment paradigm would be predicted to increase arousal and obstruct achieving therapeutic goals. However, the presence of the therapy animal should lower arousal and facilitate the learning and performance of the new behavior by counteracting stress produced by the presence of the therapist (Gerbasi, 2004). Many studies have demonstrated that the presence of therapy animals can be relaxing and stress reducing (Allen et al 2001; Allen, 2002). This decrease in arousal could facilitate the client's ability to perform a difficult or poorly learned task in the presence of a stress reducing animal and therapist as opposed to therapist only condition. Therefore, the animal's presence should counteract the increased arousal generated by the presence of the therapist.

Theoretical foundations for the application of animal assisted therapy include that of humanistic or person-centered theory from Abraham Maslow and Carl Rogers. An examination of Maslow's hierarchy of needs indicate several ways in which a client's needs may be met through AAT. Looking at each step of the hierarchical pyramid a therapist can not only assess what the client's needs are, but fashion specific therapeutic interventions to meet those needs drawing from the many tools and experiences offered through AAT. The peak or spiritual "mountaintop experiences" referred by Maslow (1970) in this hierarchy normally occurs in an environment of nature and animals. Rogers' entire theory focuses on a single "force of life" he calls the actualizing tendency (Rogers, 1951). It is the built-in motivation present in every life form to develop its potential to the fullest extent possible. We are not just talking about survival: Rogers believes that all creatures strive to make the very best of their existence. Unlike Maslow's use of the term, Rogers applies it to all living creatures.

Rogers felt that an effective therapist must have three very special qualities: 1) Congruence or genuineness; 2) Empathy; and 3) Respect or unconditional positive regard toward the client. According to Carl Rogers, the most important quality of the counseling alliance is the establishment of a warm, permissive, and accepting climate for the client (Rogers, 1951). Therapy dogs are known for the enthusiastic, warm, and affectionate greetings they give to clients (Fine, 2000; Fine, 2006). These initial encounters help to ease tension at the beginning of the meeting, and enrich the therapeutic environment. In order for therapy to be successful, clients need to feel they are in a safe environment. The client must trust their therapist before they can talk openly about their personal thoughts and experiences.

Another theoretical approach applied effectively to addiction treatment, the therapeutic alliance, and AAT is attachment theory. Addiction can be viewed as an attachment disorder (Flores, 2004) and AAT has been used as a treatment approach for attachment disorders (Terpin, 2004) and promoting social lubrication (Lefkowitz, 2005). Individuals who have difficulty establishing mature emotional attachments to other humans or even animals are more inclined to substitute drugs and alcohol for their deficiency toward intimacy. This escape to drugs can serve as a destructive coping mechanism to avoid the gnawing emptiness and internal discomfort that threatens to overwhelm them.

Attachment theory began with the study of animal attachment when Harlow (1958) discovered that infant monkeys attached to surrogate mothers when away from their real mothers. The young monkeys preferred heated, cloth covered mothers to wire mothers at all stages of development. These infant monkeys functioned better in all areas of their lives compared to others, who only had a wire mother. Young primates were more likely to be better adjusted physically, psychologically and socially compared to the monkeys raised by the wire mother. Harlow concluded that the primates are better off in their lives when given more creature comforts, attention and grooming when compared to those deprived of these elements (Harlow).

Harlow (1958) also believed that the infant monkey would form a close attachment to their surrogate cloth mothers. These surrogate mothers became a secure base when opportunities to venture out and explore came. These infants used their emotional bond to their cloth mother to ensure their safety when encountering new stimuli. When a threatening stimulus occurred, the infant retreated to the cloth mothers for safety and security. This highly correlates with Ainsworth's (1967) finding that human infants used their mothers as a secure base to explore, but periodically returning to ensure themselves that she was still there.

These and other early studies (Ainsworth, Blehar, Waters, & Wall, 1978) focused primarily on the attachment in childhood. In recent years, research has expanded to research adult attachment (Simpson & Rholes, 1998; Strauss, 2000). Adult attachment styles describe individuals' comfort and confidence in intimate relationships. It describes the fear of rejection, the yearning for closeness and the client's preference for independence and interpersonal distance (Meyer & Pilkonis, 2002).

The inability to establish long-lasting gratifying relationships correlates to the quality of early attachment experiences (Main, 1996). Those who develop dysfunctional or insecure attachment styles will be more vulnerable and more likely to turn to other sources of external modulators like substances or other obsessive-compulsive behaviors. Bonding to others, including animals are an integral part of the human condition. The stronger the earliest attachment experience, the less a person will require excessive sources of external support. Human beings who are loved and cared for by positive parenting and even healthy human-animal relationships acquire a strengthened self over the course of their development (Bartholomew & Horowitz, 1991; Bretherton & Munholland, 1999). If children have been the consistent recipient of their parents' and pets' interest and love, the more skills and confidence they will have in their capacity to evoke responsiveness from others. Accordingly, adult relationships can be more satisfying and rewarding, decreasing the likelihood that an individual would substitute substances for this needed emotional support (Flores, 2004).

Attachment theory holds the position that substance abuse is both a solution and outcome of a person's weakened ability in developing healthy attachments. If addicts or alcoholics are to achieve abstinence and sobriety, they must first detach from their destructive relationship to substances and develop the capacity for healthy interpersonal attachments. According to attachment theory, individuals are driven instinctively from birth for close human and/or animal contact (Bowlby, 1988; Baumeister & Leary, 1995). When clients are deprived of this need and do not possess the ability to accomplish this important task, individuals are emotionally deficient and vulnerable to addiction. From an attachment perspective, attachment to an animal can furnish support and emotional regulation that newly recovering alcoholics and addicts need while they make the difficult transition from detachment to alcohol to attachment to recovery. Animals can serve as both attachment figures and transitional objects (Kruger & Serpell, 2006).

Addicted and alcoholic clients are always vulnerable to compulsive, obsessive, and addictive behaviors, constantly substituting one addiction for another until variables in their life improves. Clients with addictive disorders appear to perpetually cycle through the "Stages of Change" (Prochaska, Norcross, & Diclemente, 1993) of precontemplation, contemplation, preparation, action and maintenance. However, according to attachment theory what these clients are facing is an expected cycle that many began early in childhood with insecure attachment experiences (Waters, Merrick, Treboux, Crowell, & Albersheim, 2000).

A healthy identity can only be accomplished within curative and healthy relationships. The client needs a consistent, nurturing, mirroring, and holding environment that can constrain and manage negative, destructive impulses while giving the client the opportunity to identify, internalize, and incorporate a healthy set of interpersonal social skills. When relationship skills are learned, the new self can flourish, only if, like any life form, it is in an environment that is regularly nurtured, fed, hydrated and allowed to thrive and mature (Hamilton, 2000). This can begin with the substance abuser in a strong therapeutic alliance (Mallinckrodt, Bantt, & Coble, 1995) but will only happen long-term when the client can establish and maintain healthy intimate interpersonal relationships outside of the therapeutic milieu. Until then, the lack of satisfying healthy relationships in the clients' lives may lead to feelings of emptiness and a susceptibility to search for external sources of gratification such as drugs and alcohol (Flores, 2004). The human-animal bond can serve as a bridge to allow the client to practice and learn these interpersonal skills needed for a healthy human relationship.

Within the attachment model, the goal of successful adult development is the achievement of the capacity for both intimacy and autonomy. According to Holmes (1996) Substance abusers and their spouses display fairly predictable dysfunctional patterns. The alcoholic or addict's spouse is attached to each other but not intimate. The alcoholic or addict can be neither, since his or her attachment relationship remains to the chemical. Neither can feel satisfied with themselves or the relationship (Flores, 2004). Until this pattern of selfish independence stops, difficulties will continue to plague their life and their relationships.

Alcoholics and addicts will usually not give up their chemical use until the pain and dysphoria they experience from its continual use exceed the pleasure or euphoria they gain from its present use. Conversely, the possibility of successful long-term recovery is greatly reduced unless the alcoholic's and addict's newfound life of abstinence is more rewarding than the previous one that was centered on drug and alcohol use. Alcoholics and addicts will not remain drug and alcohol free unless they derive more pleasure from a chemically free lifestyle than they did from their substance abusing lifestyle. Since addiction is compensatory in nature and driven by a lack of satisfactory attachment experiences, long-term recovery is not possible until the ability to achieve satisfaction from interpersonal attachments is achieved (Flores, 2004).

Since most addicts and alcoholics are exceedingly intolerant of delaying gratification, they usually choose a certain source of immediate gratification such as drugs and alcohol over an uncertain source of probable satisfaction in the distant future. To alter this ingrained mind-set and habitual learned pattern of behavior, they must first understand that their solution is the problem. Walant (1995) and Doherty (1995) believe that self-reliance and individuation in today's society has greatly influenced the rise in mental health and addiction problems. The reason for the increase in substance abuse in American society is due to the normal attachment needs of our children being sacrificed for cultural norms that emphasize individuation. Parental neglect occurs when parental instinct and empathy are replaced by American cultural norms, which downplay healthy interdependency. Addiction treatment should help the alcoholic and addict develop the capacity for attachment. Many in the addiction field view alcoholism as a disease of isolation. Addiction treatment should break through this seclusion and detachment from needed social support.

According to Holmes (1996) secure attachment can liberate the addict by opening a new world to a person enslaved by isolation or codependency. This is true for the securely attached child as it is for the securely attached client who has a firm therapeutic alliance with the therapist. Just as the securely attached child will move greater distances away from the caregiver, taking more risks exploring the surrounding environment, clients who have securely attached to their therapist and/or therapy animal, will take more risks in therapy, exploring their experiences more readily. Bowlby (1988) suggests normal development is not the movement from dependence to independence, but rather the movement from immature dependence to mature interdependence or mutuality. The regulatory power of mature dependence or secure attachment relationships to others including animals is necessary if substance abusers are to relinquish their reliance on the destructive dependency to substances. Independence, or more correctly the addict and alcoholic's counter dependence, is a force that fuels the substance abuser's narcissistic position and isolation, both of which are the foundation of all addiction (Flores, 2004).

The long-term goals of attachment-oriented therapy are mutuality and secure attachment, which help break the substance abuser's cycle of alienation and isolation. Secure attachment occurs once insecure and ambivalent attachment styles are relinquished (Ainsworth 1989). If long-term treatment requirements are to be successfully achieved, the substance abuser will begin to understand and experience healthy mutuality with others, which can begin through the therapeutic alliance with the therapist and animal co-therapist. Recent research indicates that there is a direct link between attachment styles and the therapeutic alliance (Eames & Roth, 2000; Kanninen, Salo, & Punamaki, 2000). It should also be noted that attachment styles of the therapist can also determine the strength of the therapeutic alliance (Tyrrell, Dozier, Teague, & Fallot, 1999), thereby influencing important aspects of process and outcome in individual adult psychotherapy (Meyer & Pilkonis, 2002).

The relationships that can develop between humans and animals are as diverse as their human counterparts (Raina, Waltner-Toews, Bonnett, Woodward, & Abernathy, 1999). At the more secure end of the attachment spectrum, the bond between human and animals can be just as strong as many human relationships. The relationships between a human and animal are forms of attachment behavior that develop between a person and an animal, involving unconditional love, security, and trust. Due to the reciprocal influences of attachment behaviors, humans can find it easier to bond to an animal that responds to them in loving and affectionate ways more than with other humans where relationships can become diffused with mixed variables (Triebenbacher, 1998). People respond positively to the animal's tendency to respond to their non-verbal cues that give them constant feedback and positive reinforcement. The human-animal attachment can help people feel loved and important, elevating their self esteem and lead to the improvement of social skills with other humans (Terpin, 2004). Human-animal attachment relationships can be so strong that it makes it reasonable to use theoretical models of human attachment theory to investigate these relationships (Bonas, McNicholas, & Collis, 2000).

Ninety-eight percent of children and adolescents studied by Eckstein (2000) loved their pets. Bowlby (1969) first defined attachment as a lasting psychological connectedness between others, which require several key concepts. One component involves the concept that relationships act as secure bases for individuals to explore the world and grow emotionally (Raupp, Barlow, & Oliver, 1997). Another concept states that attachment includes a strong emotional connectedness to another (Raupp et al.). Pets serve as transitional object beings, helping a child to reduce anxiety while they explore their environment, play, and separate from their parents (Eckstein, 2000). Pets are better attachment objects than blankets or stuffed animals for toddlers or school-aged children (Triebenbacher, 1998) and can be attachment objects for teens and adults. Animals can encourage caring and affection toward others by providing security and comfort (Terpin, 2004).

Raupp (1999) supports the concept of attachment as a part of the relationship between humans and pets because individuals often view pets as part of their family. Many people emotionally bond to their pet and grieve when they die. Individuals accept responsibility for their pets and share their lives with their pets. The bond between humans and animals can be very strong; simpler than human-to-human attachments and less conflictual, promoting fewer opportunities for insecure attachment styles (Terpin, 2004). Pets have the potential to provide a secure attachment bond that promotes a sense of security and wellness (Sable, 1995).

Vidovic, Stetic, and Bratko (1999) study concluded that children who owned pets and scored high on pet attachment scales displayed significantly higher levels of empathy and prosocial behaviors than their non-pet owners and scored low on pet attachment. This study and others (Melson, 1990; Paul, 2000) suggest that the mere presence of an animal can produce positive change in interpersonal relationships with others.

The Need for Empirical Research

One intervention with increasing promise is that of animal assistedtherapy (AAT). Unfortunately, few controlled quantitative studies exist showing the therapeutic effectiveness of formal animal assistedtherapy programs (Wilson & Barker, 2003). Much of the research that has espoused the benefits of AAT has been based on anecdotal success or limited or poor data. Another common criticism of AAT is that goals are not identified and therefore too often allowing imprecise evaluations (Beck, 2000). Scholars have discussed difficulties of research in the field and call for better research (Johnson, et al, 2002 & Odendaal, 2002; Wilson, 2006).

A recent meta-analysis by Barba (1995) revealed that of 52 research articles from the period of 1988 to 1993 on AAT most studies were nonexperimental with nonprobability, nongeneralizable samples. Garrity and Stallones (1998) identified 25 empirically based AAT studies between 1990 and 1995. Only five of the 25 studies were experimental in nature with appropriate designs to address causation (Wilson and Barker, 2003). There have been numerous studies over the last three decades on AAT; however, most of them have not been well-controlled studies. Gerbasi (2004) found that only one study (Zisselman et al, 1996) of the 128 articles described in her analysis used random assignment of subjects to treatment conditions AND blind scoring of data. "Clearly, the gold standard for research of this type is to have a random assignment to an AAT format and a traditional therapy format and then to determine which format led to a better therapeutic outcome" (Fine & Mio, 2006, p. 517).

There is a need for evidence-based research for AAT interventions. Substantive empirical evidence does not exist to support the use of AAT with the adult substance abuse population. This literature review only indicates how a therapy dog can improve the social climate of an institution, which could include a residential substance abuse treatment center, used in this study. In the next chapter, the structure of this current quantitative study is explained.

CHAPTER 3
METHODOLOGY

Introduction

The purpose of this study was to evaluate the relationship of Animal Assisted Therapy (AAT) on the therapeutic alliance with an adult residential substance abuse population in group therapy. This chapter will detail the specific research questions and the hypothesis for this study. Details will be provided regarding the role of the therapist, therapy animal, facility, study instruments, researcher, and the study participants. Finally, the procedures for data collection and analysis are included.

This quantitative study includes an experimental design using randomized populations and controlled conditions to establish the effects of chosen variables that influence outcome. This study attempts to account for all known principal variables, yet even the most rigorous experimental designs are subject to intervening variables that are outside of the researcher's control (Barker, Best, Fredrickson, & Hunter, 2000).

This present study contributes to the literature of AAT and more specifically to research the effects of AAT on the therapeutic alliance in a group setting among an adult population of residential substance abuse clients. To make the study more applicable for replicability, specific information is provided about the animal and the handler/therapist involved in the study.

Research Questions

1.   Does AAT make a positive difference in the therapeutic alliance as measured on the Helping Alliance Questionnaire (HAQ-II) for a sample of adult clients in residential substance abuse treatment in a group therapy session?

2.   Does AAT make a positive difference in lowering stress as measured by heart and blood pressure rates for a sample of adult clients in residential substance abuse treatment in a group therapy session?

Research Hypotheses

1.   Clients in an AAT group session will show higher ratings of the therapeutic alliance, as measured on the Helping Alliance Questionnaire (HAQ-II), over clients in a group therapy session without the therapy dog present.

2.   Client in an AAT group session will demonstrate lowered stress levels, as measured by lowered blood pressure (diastolic and systolic) and heart rate over clients in a group therapy session without the therapy dog present.

The Researcher, Therapist, Animal, and Setting

Different animals have different impacts on human health (Friedmann, 2000). AAT significance may be based, in part, on past experiences of the client with animals and their beliefs and fears about specific breeds and species. Past pet exposure and pet ownership all play a significant role in the effects the animal will have on the client. The individual's gender, ethnicity, and other factors can all be influence on the impact animals can have in therapy (Brown, 2002). For example, evidence exists showing how animal interaction can improve cardiovascular health (Anderson, Reid, & Jennings, 1992; Dembicki & Anderson, 1996), but when dogs were compared with cats, increased survival rates were not seen for cat owners (Friedmann & Thomas, 1995). Indeed in one study, Rajack (1997), found that cat owners were more likely to be readmitted to the hospital for cardiac problems than were dog owners. Dogs alone may be important to many health benefits and improved social interaction with others (McNicholas & Collis, 2000; Wells, 2004).

Therapy animal certification is necessary to ensure the best possible outcome and safety for the client, therapist and animal. To become a Pet Partner® therapy animal, specific prerequisites must be met and training and testing completed (Delta Society, 2005). First, the animal must pass the required health screenings and be from a breed and training that does not impose a recognized threat to clients. Training includes electing and preparing animals for visits, identification and decreasing stress in animals, animal and client health and safety, facility health and safety codes and much more. Finally, the animal and handler must pass two tests, a skills test to show whether the animal can be controlled and the aptitude test designed to simulate conditions that may be encountered on a therapy visits (Delta Society).

The certified therapy animal for this study was a Beagle mix dog named Mitzi Ann. Her handler and owner, Neresa Minatrea, was a doctoral level therapist conducting the group sessions for this study. Mitzi Ann had been abandoned in a garage with a litter of puppies in May 1999. Shortly thereafter Mitzi Ann adopted her new family while living in the local city humane society shelter. She weighs 27 pounds, and stands 17 inches high at the shoulder. At the time of this study, she was estimated to be approximately 7 years old. Mitzi Ann quickly demonstrated her skills by providing comfort, service, and nurture to Neresa Minatrea during her own struggles with ovarian cancer. To enhance this training, Mitzi Ann completed three 10-week sessions of advance obedience training, and three 8-week sessions of agility training. Mitzi Ann first earned her International Certification as a Delta Pet Partner in July 2004. Delta's test examiners qualified her to work with any mental or medical condition; all age groups; and with any environmental settings (e.g., intensive care units, hospitals, prisons, schools, physical rehabilitation units, nursing homes, treatment centers, group homes, etc.) At the beginning of this study, Mitzi had provided 87 hours of therapy in a variety of settings (e.g., adult day care centers, public schools, children's clubs, etc) and had worked with a myriad of mental and physical concerns (stroke, multiple sclerosis, autism, Down's syndrome, mental and physical challenges, etc). Mitzi has presented at community organizations (2), and state level counseling conferences (2), television (3), and for newspapers (3) demonstrating the benefits of augmenting traditional therapy with AAT or Animal Assisted Activity (AAA). Lastly, A Local Volunteer Exchange (ALIVE) organization nominated Mitzi Ann and her handler Dr. Minatrea for volunteer of the year for 2004 and for the regional volunteer of the year.

Controlling for therapeutic differences, the therapist for the experimental and the control group was the same facilitator, Dr. Neresa B. Minatrea. At the time of the study, this female therapist maintained her license as a Professional Clinical Counselor from Kentucky and held numerous national and state certifications. She was certified with Kentucky as an Alcohol and Drug Counselor and on a National certification level, she maintained the National Certified Addictions Counselor II and the National Board Certified Counselor. Lastly, Dr. Minatrea earned her certification with the International Delta Society as a Pet Partner.

Her other academic credits included a Doctoral Degree of Philosophy from the College of Education, Department of Educational Psychology at the University of South Carolina in 1996; a Master of Education from Boston University in 1985 and a Bachelors of Arts from M. H. Baylor University in 1982. She has worked 20 years post Masters in various organizations utilizing counseling, supervisory and presentation skills. Beyond her academic courses, she has presented 53 training seminars throughout the world. She currently teaches and evaluates graduate level counselors-in-training at Western Kentucky University.

While the above-mentioned credentials, experiences, and specialized training have afforded this therapist the expertise to lead these two groups, her bias toward AAT are considered and understood in this project. Many therapy dog handlers can unintentionally influence the results especially when they rate the effectiveness of AAT interventions despite objective measures (Barker et al., 2000). The therapist agreed to stay within an outlined therapy format. The therapeutic goals and therapy style for both groups were the same. The use of AAT in the experimental group was the only independent variable. However, to ensure the uniformity of the groups, the groups were videotaped and sections viewed by independent reviewers.

Six independent reviewers viewed 15-minute segments of eight random control group and eight random experimental group sessions (16 total) videotaped and placed on one four-hour DVD. Each 15-minute segment started at the 30-minute mark of the session. The reviewers were graduate students with at least 48 credit hours of professional training or licensed professionals in the field. The reviewers were given a short training session conducted by the researcher. The training included information on how to use the DVD, the Session Rating Scale (SRS), and review of a sample session. The reviewers were unaware of the hypothesis of the study.

The researcher did not have power over the reviewers as an employment supervisor. The reviewers completed one Session Rating Scale (SRS) form per session segment. The SRS was scored by summing the hash marks, measured to the nearest centimeter on each of the four lines. The total possible score was 40. The SRS mean scores for both groups was compared through a one-way ANOVA to ensure that both groups were equal and a self-fulfilling prophecy explanation of support for the hypotheses could be fundamentally dismissed. Information on the SRS is in the instrumentation section of this chapter and posted in the appendix.

The facility in which the research was conducted was located in a park setting within the city limits of Bowling Green, Kentucky with a population of approximately 50,000. Bowling Green is located in South Central Kentucky, home of a midsized university, Western Kentucky University, approximately 60 miles from Nashville, Tennessee. Bowling Green is approximately 80% Caucasian, 13% Black and 4% Hispanic and 3% other races.

The residential substance abuse building was converted from an old tuberculosis hospital. The facility in which the research was conducted is part of the community mental health agency entrusted to provide services to the indigent population in a ten county area of South Central Kentucky. The state contract for the agency requires that the facility provide services to priority populations. These priority populations include pregnant women statewide, and then clients in the ten county population who have HIV, use drug intravenously or are in drug court. Finally, the facility will admit other clients within the designated ten county area of South Central Kentucky. The facility has an approximate two-month waiting list during which a client is first assessed before a residential bed is available.

The residential treatment facility was in existence for approximately 15 years. The researcher for this study was the program manager for this facility and was hired in November 2003. Since becoming the manager, there have been numerous changes to treatment philosophy and programming. Within a year, the residential program has become more client-centered in its approach and willing to look at alternative means to increase the therapeutic alliance.

This researcher was not the therapist or dog handler in this research study. The researcher, although being a dog owner, has never been a dog handler, trainer or personally been involved directly or indirectly with AAT. This researcher attempted to remain unbiased throughout the study with only limited reading of AAT that stimulated interest in this project.

Research Participants and Participants Rights

Clients who participated in this research study must (a) have been enrolled in residential treatment at the designated facility during the research phase of this research project and needing Level III treatment (ASAM, 2001), (b) had a diagnosis of substance dependence; (c) signed a written consent form, (d) understand and communicate in English; (e) been able to attend and participate in group therapy for approximately one hour.

After acceptance by the Institutional review board on ethical standards in research and submission of the preliminary research proposal to the organization administration, permission was given to approach the eligible participants to take part in this study. The participants considered physically and emotionally stable, and presented no risk of harm to themselves or others or the animal were eligible for the study. Any group member with a history of abusing pet animals was not allowed to participate in this research project.

Randomization was used to select each of the control and experimental groups from the eligible clients. Each client had an equal opportunity to be in the experimental group. Participants placed their name on a selected piece of paper that was folded and placed in a bowl. The members for each group were randomly chosen from the blind pieces of paper in the bowl. There were 26 groups, 14 experimental groups and 12 control groups. Two control groups were removed from the analysis due to intervening variables. Each group had an approximate range of 7 to 10 members per group. Some research participants shared in more than one group but did not participate in both the control and experimental groups to avoid contamination of the research study. The unit of analysis for this study was the individual attending one group session.

Participant rights were explained in the Consent to Participate Form (Appendix A). Participants signed the form and were given a copy at their request. The study was strictly voluntary and the client was able to opt out of the study at any time. They were allowed the right to refuse to answer any questions they considered invasive or stressful. There were no known risks in participating in this study but the consent did explain potential risks and benefits. Participants were encouraged to notify the Walden University Research Participant Advocate of any adverse event. Research records were kept and continue to be strictly confidential and stored in a locked file. Only the researcher and the therapist have access to these records.

Procedures

Participants were educated on the research project. Confidentiality was assured verbally and in writing. Each willing participant was given copies of any consent upon request. Each participant was given an initial questionnaire (Appendix B) that asks for specific demographic information. They were then asked to complete the Pet Attitude Scale (Appendix C). Research participants were only then identified and randomly assigned to the experimental and control groups.

The experimental and control group sessions were conducted in the mornings. Prior to each group session, both the control and experimental group clients had their vital signs measured. After each group session, vital signs were again tested and the participants from both groups completed the Helping Alliance Questionnaire (HAQ-II, Appendix D). Group members had their vital signs taken at the nurses' station, just down the hall from the group room. The clients could wait up to eight minutes to have their vital signs read. Each group session was approximately one hour with a 15-minute break for the therapist between each group. Once the 26 sessions were complete, it marked the end of the experimental phase of the research and the beginning of the data analysis portion of the study.

Therapeutic Goals and Techniques

Choice theory (Glasser, 1998) provided the therapeutic philosophy of the cognitive-behavioral therapy used by the therapist for the experimental and control groups. The group therapy sessions had specific treatment goals. Specific treatment goals used in this study and outlined by Gammonley et al. (1997) included improving socialization, communication and reducing isolation, boredom and loneliness within the group therapy process; brighten affect and mood, lessen depression and provide pleasure and affection within the group therapy process; address grieving and loss issues if addressed within the group therapy process; improve self-esteem, opportunity to succeed and feel important and improve feeling of self-worth; improve cooperation and improve problem solving ability within the group therapy process; improve concentration and attention while increasing engagement in the group therapy process; decreasing manipulative behaviors, if applicable, in the group therapy process; improve ability to express feelings; reduce general anxiety that is common among process group therapy sessions; and reduce abusive behavior, improve ability to trust and learn about appropriate touch.

The therapist used her skills as an experienced therapist to address many of these specific goals in the process group by using specific techniques based on her chosen theory, and the needs of the client and group at the time of treatment. It was unreasonable to predict the specific techniques that were used for each group due to the specific issues that may have needed to be addressed at the time of treatment. The therapist employed the use of animal assisted therapy techniques with the experimental group based on the treatment goals of the group, which was listed above. The action of the therapy animal varied depending on the treatment goals of the group and individuals within the group. Specific AAT techniques used in this study and based on the treatment goals included the client teaching the animal something new, engaging in play with the therapy animal, receiving appropriate affection from and giving appropriate affection to the therapy animal and by generalizing animal behavior to human circumstances (Gammonley et al., 1997).

The therapy animal used in this study was trained in specific techniques that were conducive to specific group or individual treatment goals. For example, the therapy dog was trained to remove tissues from the Kleenex box and give it to any participant that cries or sneezed. The dog also naturally moved from one group participant to another, leaning in to be touched and petted. The therapy dog used a repertoire of approximately 30 tricks that were used as psychoeducational tools for the therapist within the group.

Instrumentation

Pet Attitude Scale

The Pet Attitude Scale (PAS) developed by Templer, Salter, Dickey, Baldwin, and Veleber (1981) is an 18-item Likert style form used to measure favorableness toward pets. Statistical measures include a Chronbach's alpha of .91 and test-retest reliability of .92. Construct validity was established by principal-component factor analysis and correlated with four different personality instruments in the construction and validation study.

The PAS consists of three primary factors labeled (1) love and interaction, (2) pets in home, and (3) joy of pet ownership. An individual can score a range between 38 and 266, with the higher scores indicating a more favorable attitude toward pets. Everyone eligible for this study will complete the PAS. The responses from the PAS, along with specific questions from the intake questionnaire, were used to determine participant appropriateness for this study. Clients overly fearful of animals or abused animals in the past were excluded from this study.

Session Rating Scale.

Test-retest and internal consistency reliability were evaluated by Duncan et al. (2004) using group one (N= 70). Cronbach's coefficient alpha was calculated as the estimate of internal consistency. The coefficient alpha for all administrations (N=420) was .88. The coefficient alpha for the SRS compared very well with that reported for the HAQ II (.90) despite the SRS being only a four item test and the HAQ-II having 19 items. This indicates a high degree of internal consistency. The estimate of test-retest reliability was computed by calculating the Pearson product moment correlations between the test scores at each administration. The overall test-retest reliability (Pearson *r*) for the SRS was .64, while the HAQ-II was .63. If the test-retest estimate is limited to the first and second administrations, a Pearson r of .7 is obtained for the SRS and .75 for the HAQ-II. Measures of the alliance tend to change over time, so the fact that lower test-retest reliability occurred over multiple administrations is not surprising.

Concurrent validity was computed using Pearson product-moment correlations between the SRS total score and HAQ II total score. The correlation between the two measures is .48, providing evidence of concurrent validity for the SRS. All correlations provide evidence that the SRS items are assessing the same construct as the HAQ-II and that the SRS is an ultra brief alternative for assessing global strength of the alliance similar to that measured by longer research oriented alliance measures (Duncan et al., 2004).

Helping Alliance Questionnaire (HAQ-II)

Luborsky et al. introduced The Helping Alliance Questionnaire revised (HAQ-II) in 1996. This 19-item questionnaire measures the strength of the client therapist alliance. Each item is rated on a 6-point Likert scale with 1 = *I strongly Disagree* and 6 = *I strongly Agree.* Negatively worded items are scored in reverse. This instrument has a high internal consistency (above .90 for both patient and therapist versions at sessions 2, 5 and 24), strong test-retest reliability of .79 on the patient version, and moderate to high convergent validity with the California Psychotherapy Alliance Scale (CALPAS) (Luborsky et al.). According to Duncan et al. (2004), the HAQ-II is the gold standard of alliance self-report scales.

The Initial Questionnaire

This researcher designed the initial questionnaire to obtain demographic information such as gender, race and drug of choice. One purpose for this information was to gather information to screen out individuals for the study who are high risk for being harmed in any way by AAT. The questionnaire attempted to screen out individuals who had a history of animal abuse. Some questions may appear intrusive such as questions relative to sexual orientation or legal status; however, each of the participants in this study had already answered similar and more intrusive questions to qualify for the state and federally funded services provided by this treatment provider. The data can be further used to help explain the results of the study and used as a reference for future research.

Independent and Dependent Variables

The independent variable for the research questions is the presence of a therapy dog in the substance abuse treatment group sessions within a residential treatment facility. Dependent variables measured included:

1.   The Therapeutic alliance based on HAQ-II measures.
2.   Stress levels based on vital sign measures.
   a.   Heart rate
   b.   Diastolic blood pressure rating
   c.   Systolic blood pressure rating

Data Analysis

All raw data was entered into a Microsoft Excel spreadsheet. The raw data is available upon request from the researcher. Specific raw data tables was imported in SPSS statistics software and used for all of the data analysis listed below and the graphs used in the final research paper.

Descriptive Statistics

Descriptive statistics were used to describe the basic features of the data in this quantitative study. They provide simple summaries in a manageable form about the sample population and the research variables.

ANOVA

This study made comparisons of the mean differences between groups with and without the therapy dog. A separate variance t-test and one-way analysis of variance (ANOVA) was used to compute the mean differences and test the hypothesis. A significance level of $p < .05$ was adopted for interpreting the statistical analyses of the data.

Summary

Most of the literature consists of anecdotal case studies without long-term follow-up studies or the utilization of an experimental design and statistical analyses. It was the intent of this researcher to add to the body of knowledge in the field of AAT with a well-designed quantitative study. It was hoped that research results would help to improve the practice of AAT and include its application to the substance abuse population in group therapy.

This study demanded good animal training, a high level of therapist competence, a quality treatment setting, and welfare standards for both the animal and the participants. Finally, objective measures for the program evaluation and quality assurance were used which are essential for AAT to be effective (Wilson, 2006; Fine & Mio, 2006).

CHAPTER 4
RESULTS OF THE STUDY
Introduction

The results of this study came from the measures and responses of three weeks of group sessions at the research site. All results were collected as scheduled. Although some intervening variables may have influenced the results of this study, these variables were not significant and were routine for the population and setting.

One assumption of the study was that the dog handler/therapist used in this study would not influence the experiment. To ensure the consistency of both the AAT groups and the traditional control groups, seven graduate students and/or professional therapists reviewed random samples of sessions using the Session Rating Scale (SRS). The results indicate that both the AAT groups and traditional control groups were equal without significant differences except for the therapy animal F (1, 111) .557. $p < .457$. This indicates that the self-fulfilling prophecy explanation of support for the hypotheses can largely be dismissed. Table 1 will list the results of the ANOVA and Figure 01 will display the results graphically with a means plot and error bar at the 95% confidence interval. Other potential intervening variables will be discussed in a later section.

Table 1

ANOVA and Data Analysis of Session Rating Scale Sum to Test the Self-Fulfilling Prophecy Assumption

Group	Mean (SD)
AAT Treatment [a]	31.50[c] (6.652)
Control [b]	30.57 (6.508)

[a] $N = 70$ for AAT treatment group.
[b] $N = 44$ for Control group.
[c] Mean ratings of session ratings were not statistically different $F(1, 111) .557. p < .457$.

Figure 1. Session Rating Scale mean plot and error bar at 95% confidence interval.

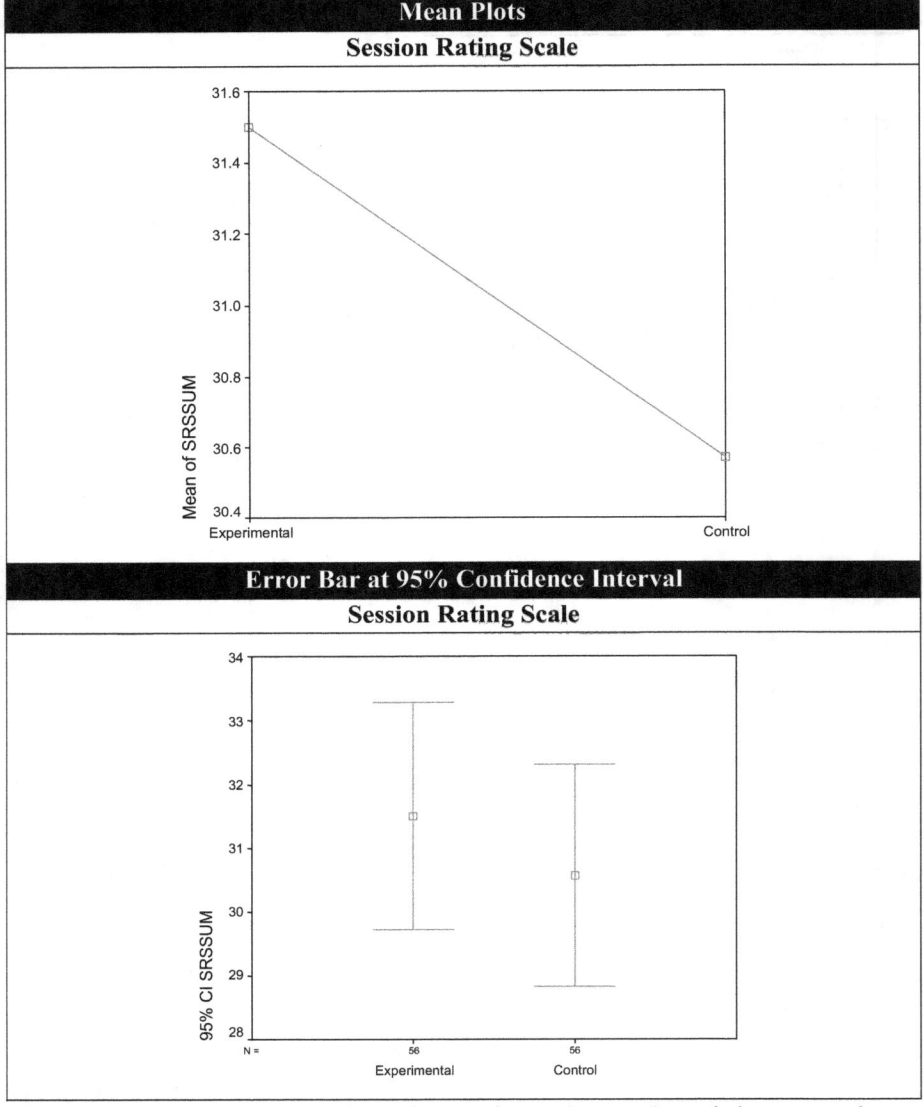

Figure 1. Mean ratings of session ratings (n = 56) and the control group (n = 56). The groups were not statistically different $F(1, 111)$ .557. $p < .457$

Population Statistics and Frequency of Responses

There were 231 individual responses from 26 group sessions. Fourteen groups were conducted for both groups. However, two control groups were removed from analysis due to contaminating factors. One group was stopped due to facility fire alarm sounding and a second due was contaminated with the therapy dog entering the group door. There were 135 HAQ-II scores and 135 presession and postsession heart rate and blood pressure outcomes from the experimental group with the therapy dog. There were 96 HAQ-II scores and 96 pre-session and post-session heart rate and blood pressure outcomes from the control group without the therapy dog.

The population was almost evenly distributed for gender with males representing 49.4% and females representing 50.6%. The population was 90.5% Caucasian and African Americans representing the remaining percentage. Over 50% of the participants were under the age of 25 and none of the participants was over the age of 55. The groups were assigned completely at random. Clients were not individually selected to take part in either group. Table 2 will give a full accounting of the population and group characteristics with frequencies and percentages listed.

The participants in this study were all seeking treatment for substance dependency in a residential treatment facility. All of the study participants were diagnosed with substance dependency to at least one substance. Approximately 69% of the population was seeking treatment for more than one substance. Many of these individuals were diagnosed with polysubstance dependence while others did not meet all of the criteria required for this diagnosis. Over 50% of the participants were seeking treatment for Alcohol (55%) and/or Methamphetamines (57.1%). Table 3 will give a full accounting of the substance abuse characteristics with frequencies and percentages listed.

The population also represented clients wanting treatment for mental health problems. More than 59% of the clients were seeking treatment for a dual diagnosis. Table 04 will give a full accounting of the mental health characteristics with frequencies and percentages listed.

Finally, the population indicated varying characteristics and attitudes related to animals and pets. Almost 70% of the participants currently owned or owned a pet within the last year. All of the clients indicated that they did not hate animals but all viewed animals or pets differently. Just over 85% of the participants believed that the primary purpose of pets is for companionship while others viewed their purpose as recreation or security and safety. Table 5 gives a full accounting of the pet history and attitude characteristics of the population with frequencies and percentages listed.

Table 2

Populations Characteristics of the Sample Population

	Population Characteristics (*N*=231)				
	Frequency		Percentage		Percentage of Both Groups
	Experimental Group	Control Group	Experimental Group	Control Group	
Age					
18 - 25	62	54	45.9	56.3	50.2
26 – 35	14	41	10.4	42.7	23.8
36 – 45	47	1	34.8	1.0	20.8
46 - 55	12	0	8.9	0.0	5.2
Total	135	96	100.0	100.0	100.0
Gender					
Male	70	44	51.9	45.8	49.4
Female	65	52	48.1	54.2	50.6
Total	135	96	100	100	100.0
Race/Ethnicity					
White/Caucasian	124	85	91.9	83.5	90.5
Black/African American	11	11	8.1	11.5	9.5
Total	135	96	100.0	100.0	100.0
Marital Status					
Single	45	70	33.3	72.9	49.8
Married	21	0	15.6	0.0	9.1
Living Together (unmarried)	14	3	14.6	3.1	7.4
Separated (not divorced)	8	0	5.9	0.0	3.5
Divorced	47	23	34.8	24.0	30.3
Total	135	96	100.0	100.0	100.0
Sexual Orientation					
Heterosexual	132	78	97.8	81.3	90.9
Homosexual	0	0	0.0	0.0	0.0
Bisexual	3	18	2.2	18.7	9.1
Total	135	96	100.0	100.0	100.0
Children					
Yes	88	72	65.2	75.0	69.3
No	47	24	34.8	25.0	30.7
Total	135	96	100.0	100.0	100.0
Highest Level of Education					
Grade School	3	13	2.2	13.5	6.9
High School	100	83	74.1	86.5	79.2
Trade School	32	0	23.7	0.0	13.9
Totals	135	96	100.0	100.0	100.0

Table continues

Population Characteristics (N=231)				
	Frequency		Percentage		Percentage
	Experimental Group	Control Group	Experimental Group	Control Group	of Both Groups
Family Annual Income					
Under $10,000	64	72	47.4	75.0	58.9
$10,000 - $20,000	21	3	.6	3.2	10.4
$20,001 - $30,000	41	3	34.4	3.2	19.0
$30,001 - $40,000	3	18	2.2	18.7	9.1
$40,001 - $50,000	6	0	4.4	0.0	2.6
Total	135	96	100.0	100.0	100.0
Court Ordered for Treatment					
Yes	99	46	73.0	48.0	62.8
No	36	50	27.0	52.0	37.2
Total	135	96	100.0	100.0	100.0
Drug Court Involvement					
Yes	2	20	1.5	20.9	9.5
No	133	76	98.5	79.1	90.5
Total	135	96	100.0	100.0	100.0
Probation or Parole					
Yes	38	69	28.1	71.9	46.3
No	97	27	71.9	28.9	53.7
Total	135	96	100.0	100.0	100.0
Social Service Involvement					
Yes	55	23	40.7	24	33.8
No	80	73	39.3	76	66.2
Total	135	96	100.0	100.0	100.0

Table 3

Substance Abuse Characteristics of the Sample Population

Substance Abuse Characteristics (*N*=231)					
	Frequency		Percentage		Percentage
	Experimental Group	Control Group	Experimental Group	Control Group	of Both Groups
Seeking Treatment for Alcohol					
Yes	85	42	63.0	43.8	55.0
No	50	54	27.0	56.2	45.0
Total	135	96	100.0	100.0	100.0
Seeking Treatment for Marijuana					
Yes	70	44	51.9	45.9	49.4
No	65	52	48.1	54.1	50.6
Total	135	96	100.0	100.0	100.0
Seeking Treatment for Methamphetamine					
Yes	85	47	63.0	49.0	57.1
No	50	49	27.0	51.0	42.9
Total	135	96	100.0	100.0	100.0
Seeking Treatment for Heroin					
Yes	9	11	6.7	11.5	8.7
No	126	85	93.3	88.5	91.3
Total	135	96	100.0	100.0	100.0
Seeking Treatment for Cocaine					
Yes	29	41	21.5	42.7	30.3
No	106	55	78.5	57.3	69.7
Total	135	96	100.0	100.0	100.0
Seeking Treatment for Rx Opiates					
Yes	45	29	33.3	30.2	32.0
No	90	67	66.7	29.8	68.0
Total	15	96	100.0	100.0	100.0
Seeking Treatment for Benzodiazepines					
Yes	9	11	6.7	11.5	8.7
No	126	85	93.3	88.5	91.3
Total	135	96	100.0	100.0	100.0
Seeking Treatment for Hallucinogens					
Yes	1	11	.08	11.5	5.2
No	134	85	99.2	88.5	94.8
Total	135	96	100.0	100.0	100.0
Seeking Treatment for more than one substance					
Yes	98	63	72.6	65.6	69.7
No	37	33	27.4	34.4	30.3
Total	135	96	100.0	100.0	100.0

Table 4
Mental Health Characteristics of the Sample Population

Mental Health Characteristics (*N*=231)					
	Frequency		Percentage		Percentage of Both Groups
	Experimental Group	Control Group	Experimental Group	Control Group	
Seeking Treatment for Dual Diagnosis					
Yes	71	65	52.6	67.7	58.9
No	64	31	47.4	36.3	41.1
Total	135	96	100.0	100.0	100.0
Seeking Treatment for Mood Disorders					
Yes	43	53	31.9	55.2	41.6
No	92	43	68.1	44.8	58.4
Total	135	96	100.0	100.0	100.0
Seeking Treatment for Anxiety Disorders					
Yes	48	54	35.6	56.6	44.2
No	87	42	64.4	43.4	55.8
Total	135	96	100.0	100.0	100.0
Seeking Treatment for Abuse History					
Yes	9	11	6.7	11.5	8.7
No	126	85	93.3	88.5	91.3
Total	135	96	100.0	100.0	100.0
Seeking Treatment for Social/Relational Problems					
Yes	23	46	17.0	47.9	29.9
No	112	50	83.0	52.1	70.1
Total	135	96	100.0	100.0	100.0
Seeking Treatment for Anger Issues					
Yes	14	34	10.4	35.4	20.8
No	121	62	89.6	64.6	79.2
Total	135	96	100.0	100.0	100.0

Table 5

Pet History and Attitudes of the Sample Population

Pet History and Attitude Characteristics (*N*=231)					
	Frequency		Percentage		Percentage
	Experimental Group	Control Group	Experimental Group	Control Group	of Both Groups
Current Pet Owner or Owner in the Past Year					
Yes	114	45	84.4	46.9	68.8
No	21	51	15.6	53.1	31.2
Total	135	96	100.0	100.0	100.0
Lost a Pet in the Last Year					
Yes	36	3	22.7	3.1	16.9
No	99	93	73.3	96.9	83.1
Total	135	96	100.0	100.0	100.0
Primary Purpose for Pet Ownership					
Companionship	121	76	89.6	79.1	85.3
Safety and Security	1	9	1.0	9.4	4.3
Recreation	13	11	9.4	11.5	10.4
Total	135	96	100.0	100.0	100.0
I really Like seeing pets enjoy their food					
Strongly Disagree	3	14	2.2	14.5	7.4
Moderately Disagree	0	0	0.0	0.0	0.0
Slightly Disagree	2	11	1.5	11.5	5.6
Unsure	11	3	8.6	3.1	6.1
Slightly Agree	5	38	3.8	39.6	18.6
Moderately Agree	36	9	26.8	9.4	19.5
Strongly Agree	78	21	57.8	21.9	42.9
Total	135	96	100.0	100.0	100.0
My pet means more to me than any of my friends					
Strongly Disagree	6	31	4.4	32.3	16.0
Moderately Disagree	0	0	0.0	0.0	0.0
Slightly Disagree	9	12	6.7	12.5	9.1
Unsure	40	11	29.6	11.5	22..1
Slightly Agree	26	21	19.3	21.9	20.3
Moderately Agree	35	20	25.0	20.8	23.8
Strongly Agree	19	1	15.0	1.1	8.7
Total	135	96	100.0	100.0	100.0
I would like a pet in my home					
Strongly Disagree	4	20	3.0	20.8	10.4
Moderately Disagree	1	9	1.0	9.4	4.3
Slightly Disagree	14	11	10.4	11.5	10.8
Unsure	13	0	9.5	0.0	5.6
Slightly Agree	27	11	20.0	11.5	16.5
Moderately Agree	12	16	8.8	16.7	12.1
Strongly Agree	64	29	47.3	30.1	40.3
Total	135	96	100.0	100.0	100.0

Table continues

	Frequency		Percentage		Percentage of Both Groups
	Experimental Group	Control Group	Experimental Group	Control Group	
Having pets is a waste of money					
Strongly Disagree	105	63	77.8	65.6	72.7
Moderately Disagree	3	22	2.2	22.9	10.8
Slightly Disagree	0	0	0.0	0.0	0.0
Unsure	13	0	9.6	0.0	5.6
Slightly Agree	12	0	8.9	0.0	5.2
Moderately Agree	0	0	0.0	0.0	0.0
Strongly Agree	2	11	1.5	11.5	5.6
Total	135	96	100.0	100.0	100.0
House pets add happiness to my life (or would if I had one)					
Strongly Disagree	2	11	1.4	11.7	5.6
Moderately Disagree	1	9	1.0	9.8	4.3
Slightly Disagree	0	0	0.0	0.0	4.8
Unsure	2	9	1.4	9.8	0.0
Slightly Agree	3	22	2.1	22.9	10.8
Moderately Agree	17	22	12.6	22.9	17.3
Strongly Agree	110	22	81.5	22.9	57.1
Total	135	96	100.0	100.0	100.0
I feel that pets should always be kept outside					
Strongly Disagree	19	24	25.0	25.0	18.6
Moderately Disagree	49	16	16.6	16.6	28.1
Slightly Disagree	47	14	14.8	14.6	26.4
Unsure	0	0	0.0	0.0	0.0
Slightly Agree	18	31	32.2	32.3	21.2
Moderately Agree	0	0	0.0	0.0	0.0
Strongly Agree	2	11	11.4	11.5	5.6
Total	135	96	100.0	100.0	100.0
I spend time every day playing with my pet (or I would if I had one)					
Strongly Disagree	2	11	1.5	11.5	5.6
Moderately Disagree	0	0	0.0	0.0	5.6
Slightly Disagree	2	9	1.5	9.4	4.8
Unsure	12	0	8.8	0.0	5.2
Slightly Agree	5	32	3.9	33.3	16.0
Moderately Agree	4	23	3.0	23.9	11.7
Strongly Agree	110	21	81.3	21.9	56.7
Total	135	96	100.0	100.0	100.0

Table title: **Pet History and Attitude Characteristics (*N*=231)**

Table continues

Pet History and Attitude Characteristics (N=231)					
	Frequency		Percentage		Percentage
	Experimental Group	Control Group	Experimental Group	Control Group	of Both Groups
I have occasionally communicated with my pet and understood what it was trying to express					
Strongly Disagree	2	11	1.5	11.5	5.6
Moderately Disagree	0	0	0.0	0.0	0.0
Slightly Disagree	12	0	8.9	0.0	5.2
Unsure	19	29	14.1	30.2	20.8
Slightly Agree	22	33	16.3	34.3	23.8
Moderately Agree	15	11	11.1	11.5	11.3
Strongly Agree	65	12	48.1	12.5	33.3
Total	135	96	100.0	100.0	100.0
The world would be a better place if people would stop spending so much time caring for their pets and started caring more for other human beings instead					
Strongly Disagree	48	12	35.6	12.5	26.0
Moderately Disagree	33	27	24.4	28.2	26.6
Slightly Disagree	22	0	16.3	0.0	9.5
Unsure	14	23	10.4	24.0	16.0
Slightly Agree	3	20	2.2	20.8	10.0
Moderately Agree	13	3	9.6	3.1	6.9
Strongly Agree	2	11	1.5	11.5	5.6
Total	135	96	100.0	100.0	100.0
I like to feed animals out of my hand					
Strongly Disagree	0	0	0.0	0.0	0.0
Moderately Disagree	0	0	0.0	0.0	0.0
Slightly Disagree	2	11	1.5	11.5	27.3
Unsure	2	9	1.5	9.4	7.4
Slightly Agree	2	11	1.5	11.5	19.0
Moderately Agree	17	29	12.6	30.1	26.0
Strongly Agree	112	36	83.0	37.5	20.3
Total	135	96	100.0	100.0	100.0
I love pets					
Strongly Disagree	0	0	0.0	0.0	0.0
Moderately Disagree	0	0	0.0	0.0	0.0
Slightly Disagree	2	11	1.5	11.5	5.6
Unsure	2	9	1.5	9.3	4.8
Slightly Agree	2	11	1.5	11.5	5.6
Moderately Agree	17	29	12.6	30.2	19.9
Strongly Agree	112	36	82.9	37.5	64.1
Total	135	96	100.0	100.0	100.0

Table continues

Pet History and Attitude Characteristics (N=231)					
	Frequency		Percentage		Percentage
	Experimental Group	Control Group	Experimental Group	Control Group	of Both Groups
Animals belong in the wild or in zoos, but not in the home					
Strongly Disagree	68	35	50.3	36.5	44.6
Moderately Disagree	21	27	15.5	28.1	20.8
Slightly Disagree	30	22	22.1	22.9	22.5
Unsure	1	3	1.0	3.1	1.7
Slightly Agree	13	0	9.6	0.0	5.6
Moderately Agree	2	9	1.5	9.4	4.8
Strongly Agree	0	0	0.0	0.0	0.0
Total	135	96	100.0	100.0	100.0
If you keep pets in the house you can expect a lot of damage to furniture					
Strongly Disagree	10	10	7.4	10.4	8.7
Moderately Disagree	3	22	2.2	22.9	10.8
Slightly Disagree	25	24	18.5	25.0	21.2
Unsure	16	18	11.9	18.7	14.7
Slightly Agree	56	0	41.5	0.0	24.2
Moderately Agree	23	11	17.0	11.5	14.7
Strongly Agree	2	11	1.5	1.5	5.6
Total	135	96	100.0	100.0	100.0
I like house pets					
Strongly Disagree	2	11	1.4	11.5	5.6
Moderately Disagree	1	11	1.0	11.5	5.2
Slightly Disagree	2	11	1.4	11.5	5.6
Unsure	2	9	1.4	9.4	4.8
Slightly Agree	42	19	31.1	19.6	26.4
Moderately Agree	43	9	31.8	9.4	22.5
Strongly Agree	43	26	31.8	27.1	29.9
Total	135	96	100.0	100.0	100.0
Pets are fun but it's not worth the trouble of owning one					
Strongly Disagree	46	15	34.1	15.6	26.4
Moderately Disagree	56	47	41.5	49.0	44.6
Slightly Disagree	33	34	24.4	35.4	29.0
Unsure	0	0	0.0	0.0	0.0
Slightly Agree	0	0	0.0	0.0	0.0
Moderately Agree	0	0	0.0	0.0	0.0
Strongly Agree	0	0	0.0	0.0	0.0
Total	135	96	100.0	100.0	100.0

Table continues

	Frequency		Percentage		Percentage of Both Groups
	Experimental Group	Control Group	Experimental Group	Control Group	
Pet History and Attitude Characteristics (N=231)					
I frequently talk to my pet					
Strongly Disagree	4	18	3.1	18.8	9.5
Moderately Disagree	13	0	9.6	0.0	5.6
Slightly Disagree	2	11	1.6	1.5	5.6
Unsure	1	3	1.1	3.1	1.7
Slightly Agree	16	20	11.9	20.8	15.6
Moderately Agree	6	29	48.9	30.2	41.1
Strongly Agree	33	15	24.4	15.6	20.8
Total	135	96	100.0	100.0	100.0
I hate animals					
Strongly Disagree	135	96	100.0	100.0	100.0
Moderately Disagree	0	0	0.0	0.0	0.0
Slightly Disagree	0	0	0.0	0.0	0.0
Unsure	0	0	0.0	0.0	0.0
Slightly Agree	0	0	0.0	0.0	0.0
Moderately Agree	0	0	0.0	0.0	0.0
Strongly Agree	0	0	0.0	0.0	0.0
Total	135	96	100.0	100.0	100.0
You should treat your house pets with as much respect as you would a human member of your family					
Strongly Disagree	2	11	1.6	1.5	5.6
Moderately Disagree	0	0	0	0	0.0
Slightly Disagree	26	0	19.5	0	11.3
Unsure	0	0	0	0	0.0
Slightly Agree	34	3	25.3	3.1	16.0
Moderately Agree	8	45	5.4	46.9	22.9
Strongly Agree	65	37	48.2	38.5	44.2
Total	15	96	100.0	100.0	100.0

HAQ-II Results and the Therapeutic Alliance

After each group session with or without the therapy dog present, the participants would rate their interpretation of the therapeutic alliance with completion of the HAQ-II questionnaire. A significant difference was found between mean HAQ-II ratings, F (1, 229) 25.44, $p < .001$, $\eta^2 = .100$, with those in the AAT groups reporting a more positive opinion of the therapeutic alliance. A review of the effect sizes calculated for the variable suggests that the addition of AAT therapy contributed most to the differences observed for mean HAQ-II ratings. Table 6 will list the results of the ANOVA. Figure 2 helps graphically demonstrate the results of this finding.

This finding confirms the hypothesis that the experimental group with the therapy dog would result in significantly higher ratings of a positive therapeutic alliance than the control group without the therapy dog present. The results indicate that the therapeutic alliance is enhanced with the addition of a therapy dog within a group setting with adult clients in a residential drug abuse treatment setting. Further discussion of this finding will be listed in a subsection to follow.

Vital Sign Indicators of Stress

Participant vital signs (heart rate and blood pressure rates) were measured before and after each group session for both the experimental and control groups. The results indicate significant differences between clients in AAT groups and control groups for two of the three vital sign dependent variables assessed. Significant differences were not found for the systolic blood pressure change but were found for the average change in heart rate, $F(1, 229)$ 13.05, $p < .001$, $\eta^2 = .054$; and the average change in diastolic blood pressure, $F(1, 229)$ 3.92, $p < .049$, $\eta^2 = .017$. In these cases, clients in the AAT groups experienced greater decreases in their vital signs (heart rate and diastolic blood pressure) than those in the groups that did not utilize AAT. A review of the effect sizes calculated for each variable suggests that the addition of AAT therapy contributed most to the differences observed for mean dependant variables. Table 7 will list the results of each ANOVA statistic. Table 3 helps graphically demonstrate the results of these findings.

The findings for both the heart rate and diastolic blood pressure both confirms the hypothesis that the experimental group with the therapy dog would result in significantly lower scores than the control group without the therapy dog present. The results indicate that two of three indicators of reduced stress levels are significantly lowered with the addition of a therapy dog within a group setting with adult clients in a residential drug abuse treatment setting. Further discussion of these findings will be listed in a subsection to follow.

Table 6.

Means, Standard Deviations, and One-Way Analyses of Variance (ANOVA) for Effects of Animal Assisted Therapy on Four Dependent Variables

Variable	Animal-Assisted Group [a]		Control Group [b]		ANOVA	
	M	SD	M	SD	F	η^2
HAQ-II Rating*	112.07	9.49	104.52	13.25	25.44	.100
Change in Pulse Rate*	-6.20	9.09	-1.54	10.39	13.05	.054
Change in Systolic Blood Pressure	-1.27	9.89	0.36	9.74	1.55	.007
Change in Diastolic Blood Pressure*	0.00	8.27	2.27	9.03	3.92	.017

[a] $N = 135$ for AAT treatment group.

[b] $N = 96$ for Control group.

*significant at $p < .05$

Figure 2. Mean plot and error bar for HAQ-II results and the therapeutic alliance.

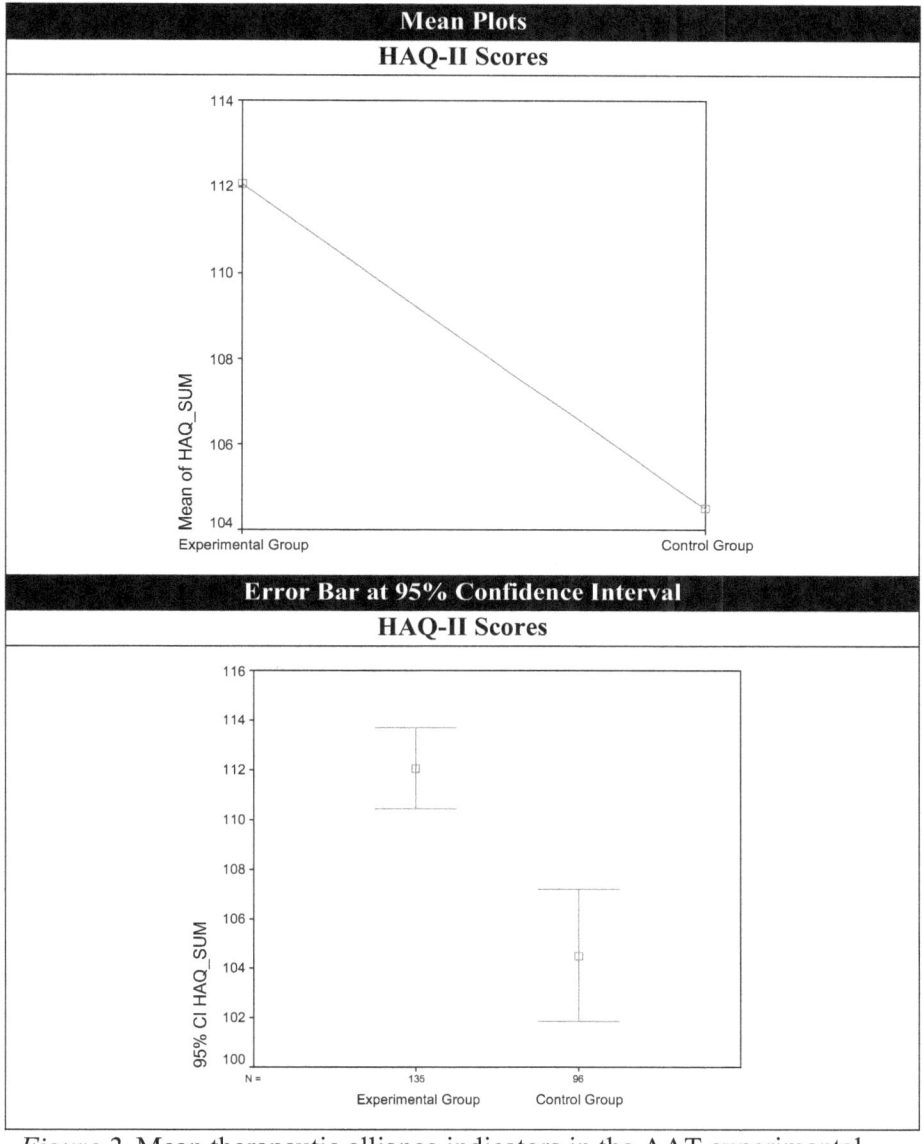

Figure 2. Mean therapeutic alliance indicators in the AAT experimental group (n = 135) and the control group (n = 96). The AAT experimental group had higher scores than the control group and was statistically significant F (1, 229) 25.44, $p < .001$, $\eta^2 = .100$

Figure 3. Mean plots and error bars for vital sign indicators of stress.

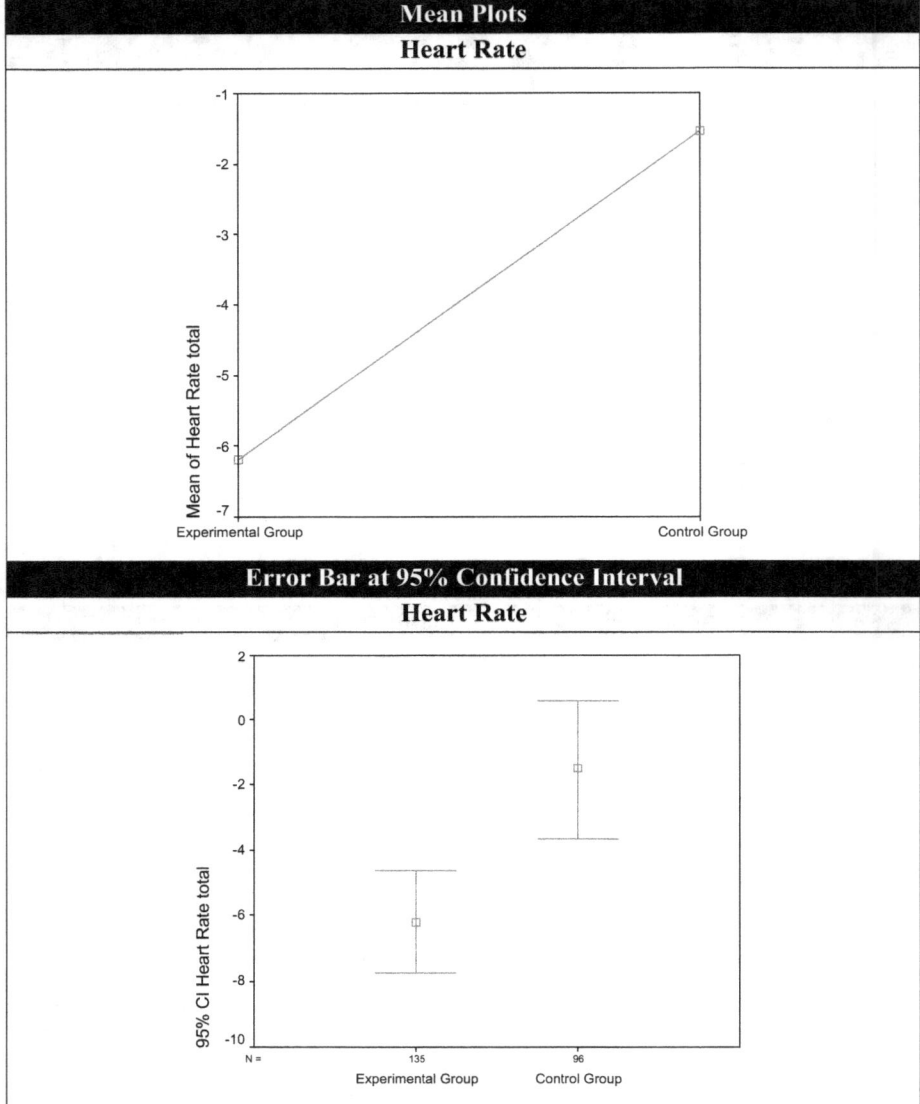

Figure 3. Mean heart rate, diastolic and systolic blood pressure indicators in the AAT experimental group (n = 135) and the control group (n = 96). The AAT experimental group had lower mean heart rates $F(1, 229)$ 13.05, $p < .001$

Figure continues

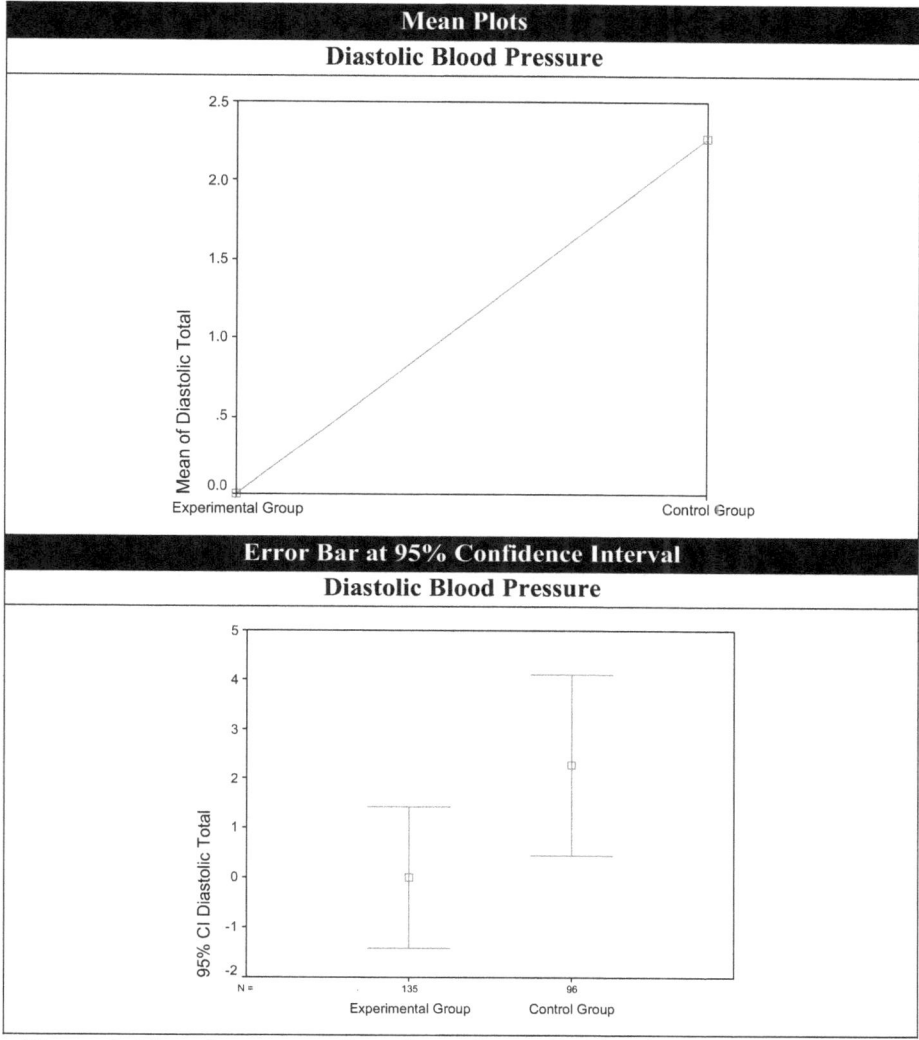

Figure 3. Mean heart rate, diastolic and systolic blood pressure indicators in the AAT experimental group (n = 135) and the control group (n = 96). The AAT experimental group had lower diastolic measures $F(1, 229)$ 3.92, $p < .049$.

Figure continues

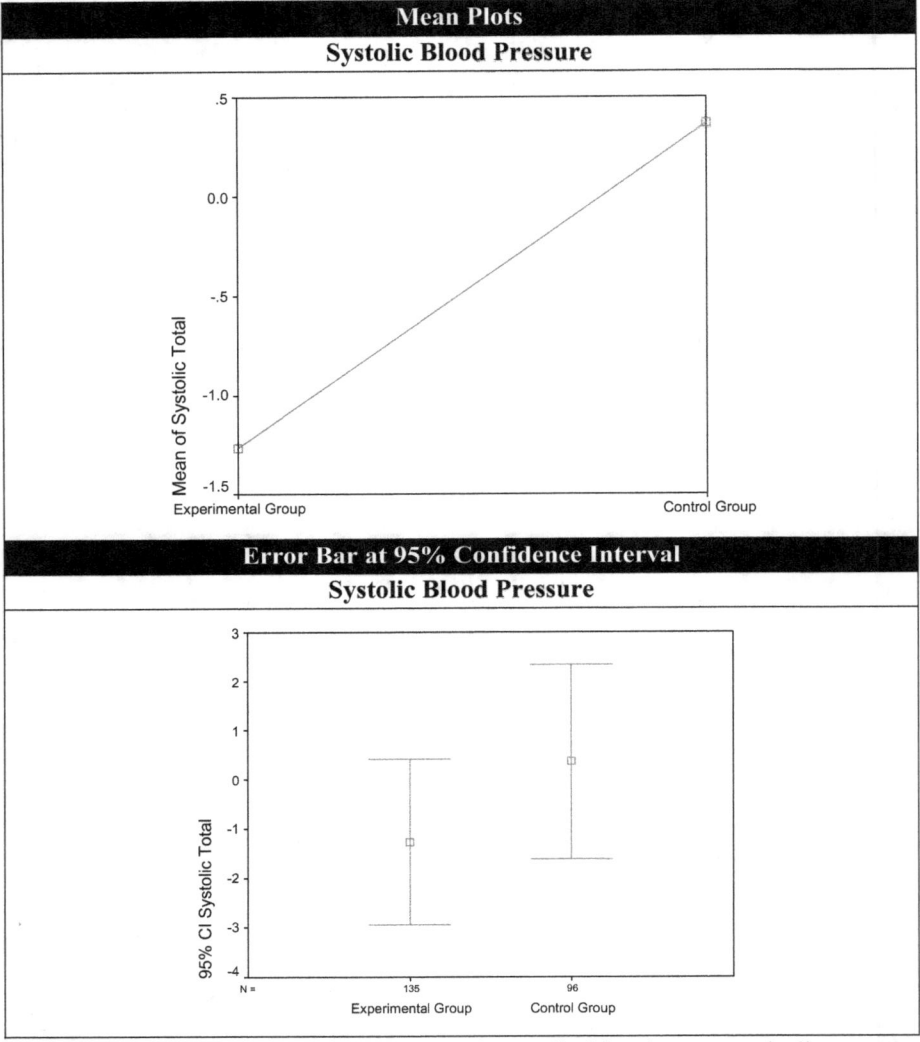

Figure 3. Mean heart rate, diastolic and systolic blood pressure indicators in the AAT experimental group (n = 135) and the control group (n = 96). The difference in systolic rates was not statistically significant $F(1, 229)$ 1.54, $p < .215$.

Population Subgroups and the Therapeutic Alliance

Once the original research questions were answered, other questions arose from the demographic data. Specific population subgroups with enough statistical power were further tested to determine if AAT would make a positive difference in the therapeutic alliance as measured on the Helping Alliance Questionnaire (HAQ-II) with the two groups. Demographic population subgroups further tested included:

1. Gender: Male and Female

2. Court Ordered Clients

3. Clients with Social Service (Child Protective Service) Involvement

4. Pet Owners

5. Dual Diagnosis Clients

6. Drug Dependence: Polysubstance, Alcohol, Marijuana and Methamphetamines

The results of this inquiry were mixed. All populations subgroups indicated significant results between the AAT group and control group except for dual diagnosis clients $F(1, 134)$ .130, $p > .719$; clients with social service (child protective service) involvement $F(1, 76)$ .062, $p > .804$; and clients seeking treatment for alcohol $F(1, 125)$ 2.91, $p > .091$. The remaining population subgroups tested found that clients in the AAT groups reported a more positive opinion of the therapeutic alliance than did individuals in the group without the therapy dog present. A significant difference was found between mean HAQ-II ratings for males, $F(1, 112)$ 34.62, $p < .000$; females $F(1, 115)$ 4.75, $p < .031$; court ordered clients $F(1, 143)$ 37.16, $p < .000$; Pet owners $F(1, 157)$ 40.59, $p < .000$; polysubstance dependence clients $F(1, 159)$ 27.85, $p < .000$; cannabis dependence clients $F(1, 112)$ 24.96, $p < .000$; and clients seeking treatment for methamphetamine dependence $F(1, 130)$ 29.57, $p < .000$; with those in the AAT groups reporting a more positive opinion of the therapeutic alliance.

Tables 8-17 will list the results of each ANOVA statistic. Figure 4 helps graphically demonstrate the results of these findings.

Table 7

Mean Therapeutic Alliance Scores by Individual Males With and Without AAT in Group

Therapy

Group	Mean (SD)
AAT Treatment [a]	110.21[c] (10.507)
Control [b]	98.25 (10.666)

[a] $N = 70$ for AAT treatment group.
[b] $N = 44$ for Control group.
[c] Mean for AAT group is higher than the Control group, significant at p < .05, the one-way analysis of variance (ANOVA), $F(1, 112)$ 34.62, $p < .000$.

Table 8

Mean Therapeutic Alliance Scores by Individual Females With and Without AAT in Group

Therapy

Group	Mean (SD)
AAT Treatment [a]	114.06[c] (7.872)
Control [b]	109.83 (10.666)

[a] $N = 65$ for AAT treatment group.
[b] $N = 52$ for Control group.
[c] Mean for AAT group is higher than the Control group, significant at p < .05, the one-way analysis of variance (ANOVA), $F(1, 115)$ 4.75, $p < .031$.

Table 9

Mean Therapeutic Alliance Scores by Court Ordered Individuals With and Without AAT

in Group Therapy

Group	Mean (SD)
AAT Treatment [a]	113.30[c] (8.283)
Control [b]	102.24 (13.394)

[a] $N = 99$ for AAT treatment group.

[b] $N = 46$ for Control group.

[c] Mean for AAT group is higher than the Control group, significant at p < .05, the one-way analysis of variance (ANOVA), $F(1, 143)$ 37.16, $p < .000$.

Table 10

Mean Therapeutic Alliance Scores by Individual Pet Owners With and Without AAT in

Group Therapy

Group	Mean (*SD*)
AAT Treatment [a]	114.09[c] (7.845)
Control [b]	104.76 (9.432)

[a] $N = 114$ for AAT treatment group.

[b] $N = 45$ for Control group.

[c] Mean for AAT group is higher than the Control group, significant at p < .05, the one-way analysis of variance (ANOVA), $F(1, 157)$ 40.59, $p < .000$.

Table 11

Mean Therapeutic Alliance Scores by Dual Diagnosis Individuals With and Without AAT in Group Therapy

Group	Mean (SD)
AAT Treatment [a]	110.31[c] (10.677)
Control [b]	109.62 (11.767)

[a] $N = 71$ for AAT treatment group.
[b] $N = 65$ for Control group.
[c] Mean for AAT group was not higher than the Control group, significant at p < .05, the one-way analysis of variance (ANOVA), $F(1, 134)$ .130, $p >$ .719.

Table 12

Mean Therapeutic Alliance Scores by Individuals with Social Service Involvement, With and Without AAT in Group Therapy

Group	Mean (SD)
AAT Treatment [a]	112.09[c] (9.252)
Control [b]	112.61 (5.639)

[a] $N = 55$ for AAT treatment group.

[b] $N = 23$ for Control group.

[c] Mean for AAT group was not higher than the Control group, significant at p < .05, the one-way analysis of variance (ANOVA), $F(1, 76)$ .062, $p >$ .804.

Table 13

Mean Therapeutic Alliance Scores by Polysubstance Dependent Individuals With and Without AAT in Group Therapy

Group	Mean (SD)
AAT Treatment [a]	113.80[c] (8.719)
Control [b]	104.86 (12.777)

[a] $N = 98$ for AAT treatment group.

[b] $N = 63$ for Control group.

[c] Mean for AAT group is higher than the Control group, significant at p < .05, the one-way analysis of variance (ANOVA), $F(1, 159)$ 27.85, $p < .000$.

Table 14

Mean Therapeutic Alliance Scores by Alcohol Dependent Individuals With and Without AAT in Group Therapy

Group	Mean (SD)
AAT Treatment [a]	111.41[c] (9.761)
Control [b]	108.40 (8.445)

[a] $N = 85$ for AAT treatment group.

[b] $N = 42$ for Control group.

[c] Mean for AAT group is not higher than the Control group, significant at p $< .05$, the one-way analysis of variance (ANOVA), $F(1, 125)$ 2.91, $p > .091$.

Table 15

Mean Therapeutic Alliance Scores by Cannabis Dependent Individuals
With and Without AAT in Group Therapy

Group	Mean (SD)
AAT Treatment [a]	114.46[c] (7.579)
Control [b]	102.80 (17.058)

[a] $N = 70$ for AAT treatment group.
[b] $N = 44$ for Control group.
[c] Mean for AAT group is higher than the Control group, significant at p < .05, the one-way analysis of variance (ANOVA), $F(1, 112)$ 24.96, $p < .000$.

Table 16

Mean Therapeutic Alliance Scores by Methamphetamine Dependent Individuals With and Without AAT in Group Therapy

Group	Mean (SD)
AAT Treatment [a]	113.15[c] (8.831)
Control [b]	102.81 (12.926)

[a] $N = 85$ for AAT treatment group.
[b] $N = 47$ for Control group.
[c] Mean for AAT group is higher than the Control group, significant at p < .05, the one-way analysis of variance (ANOVA), $F(1, 130)$ 29.57, $p < .000$.

Figure 4. Mean plots and error bars of subgroups and the therapeutic alliance

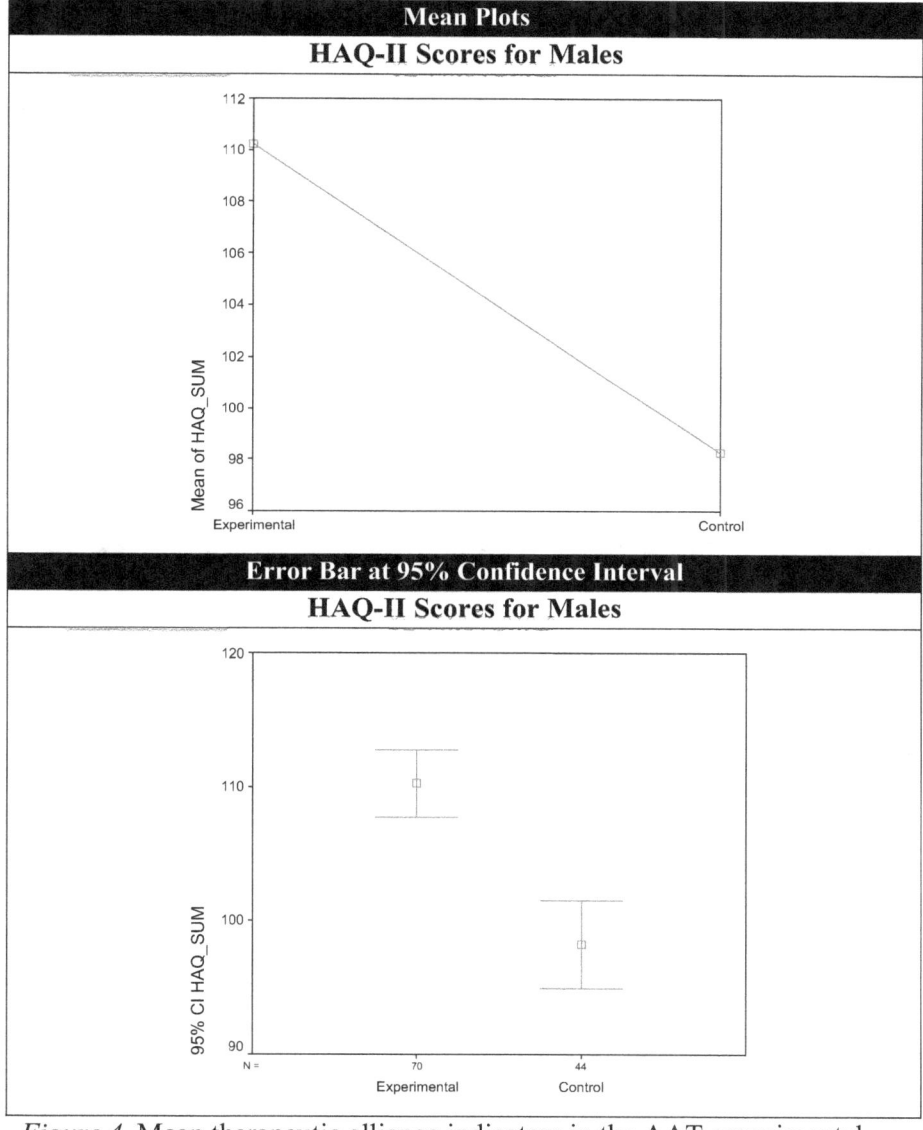

Figure 4. Mean therapeutic alliance indicators in the AAT experimental group (n = 135) and the control group (n = 96) separated into by specific subgroups. The AAT experimental group had higher alliance rates for males $F(1, 112)$ 34.62, $p < .000$.

Figure continued

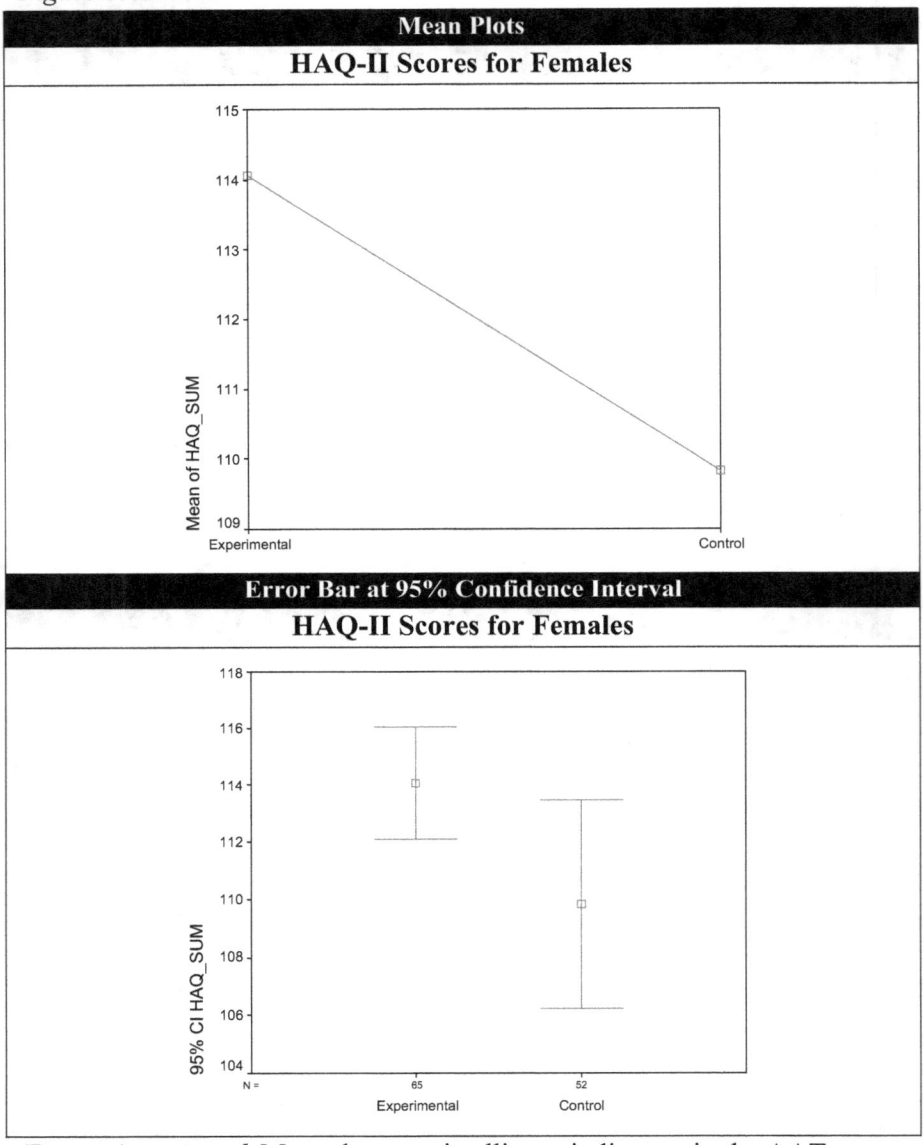

Figure 4 continued. Mean therapeutic alliance indicators in the AAT experimental group (n = 135) and the control group (n = 96) separated into by specific subgroups. The AAT experimental group had higher alliance rates for females $F(1, 115)$ 4.75, $p < .031$.

Figure continued

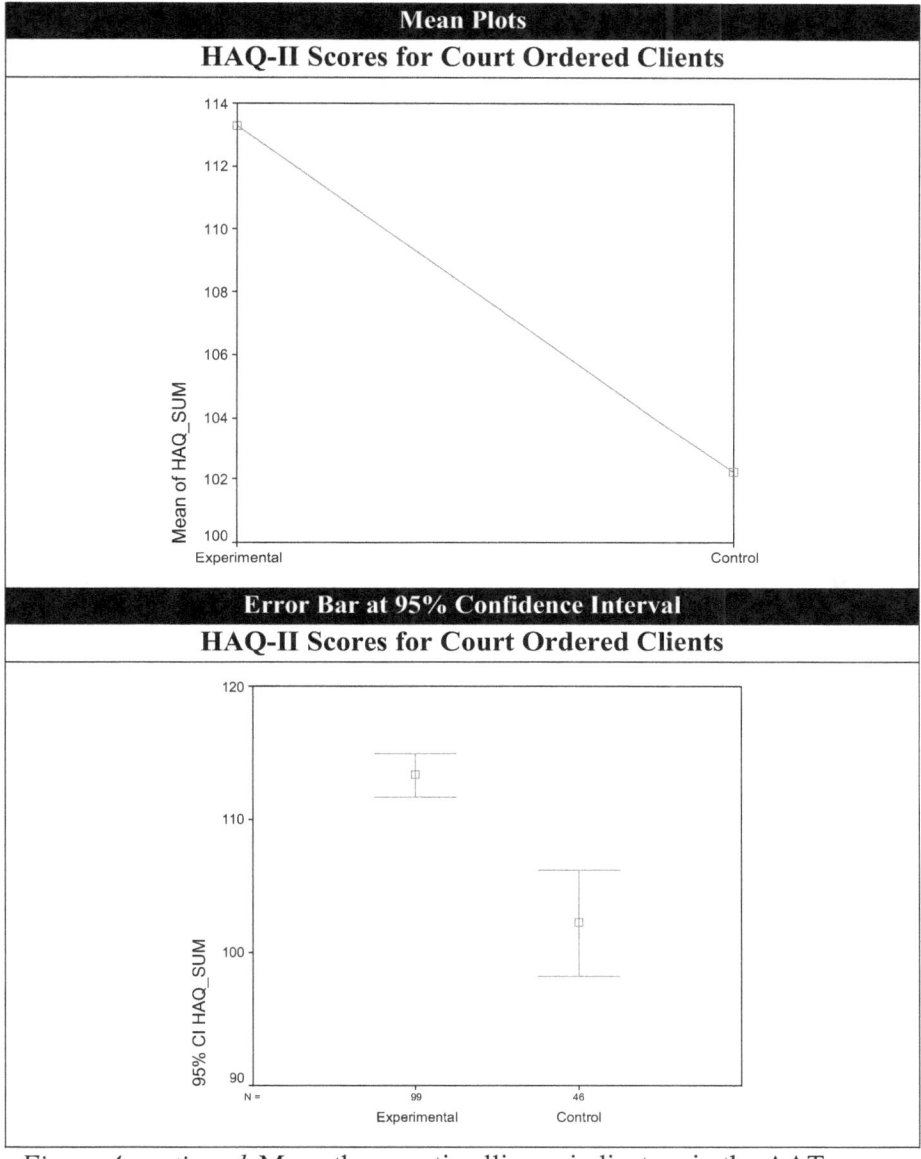

Figure 4 continued. Mean therapeutic alliance indicators in the AAT experimental group (n = 135) and the control group (n = 96) separated into by specific subgroups. The AAT experimental group had higher alliance rates for court ordered clients $F(1, 143)$ 37.16, $p < .000$.

Figure continued

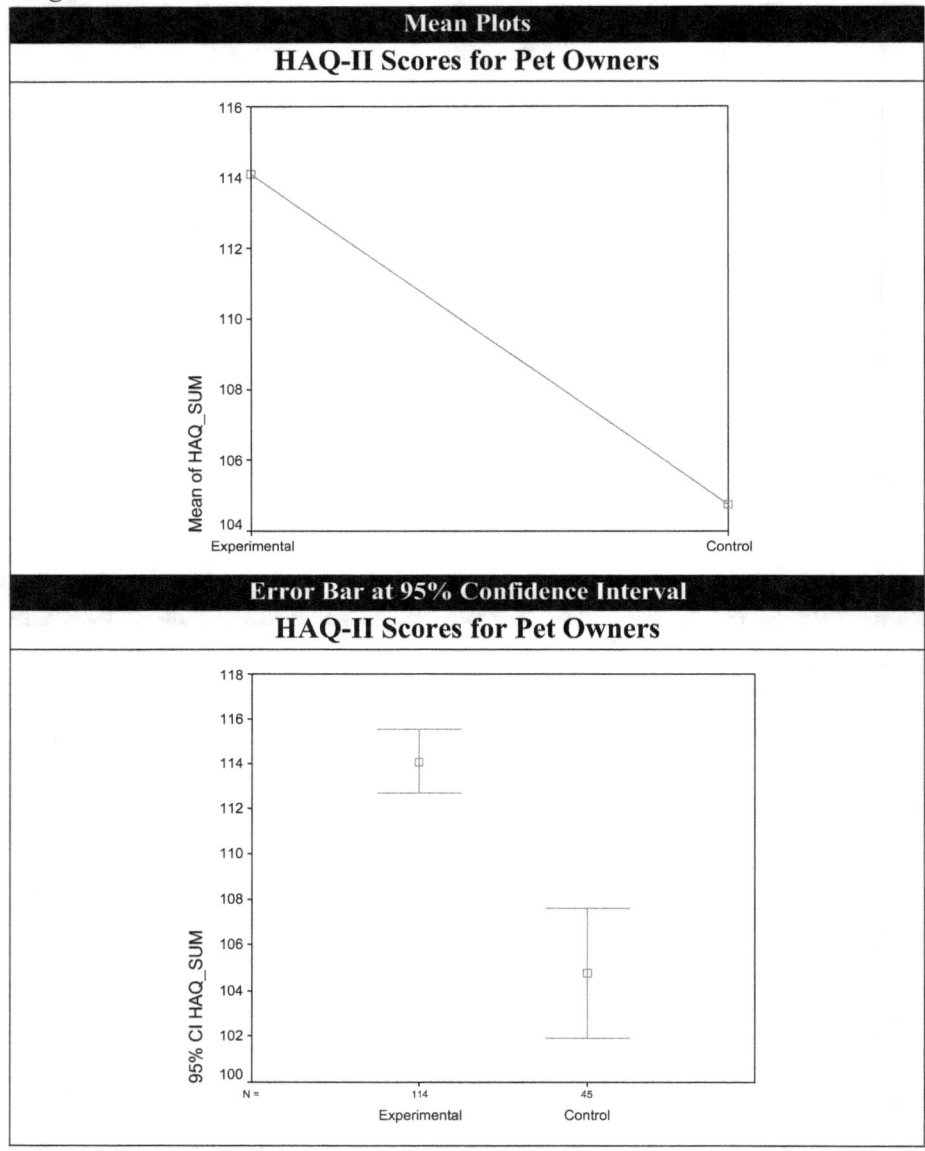

Figure 4 continued. Mean therapeutic alliance indicators in the AAT group (n = 135) and the control group (n = 96) separated into by specific subgroups. The AAT experimental group had higher alliance rates for pet owners $F(1, 157)$ 40.59, $p < .000$.

Figure continued

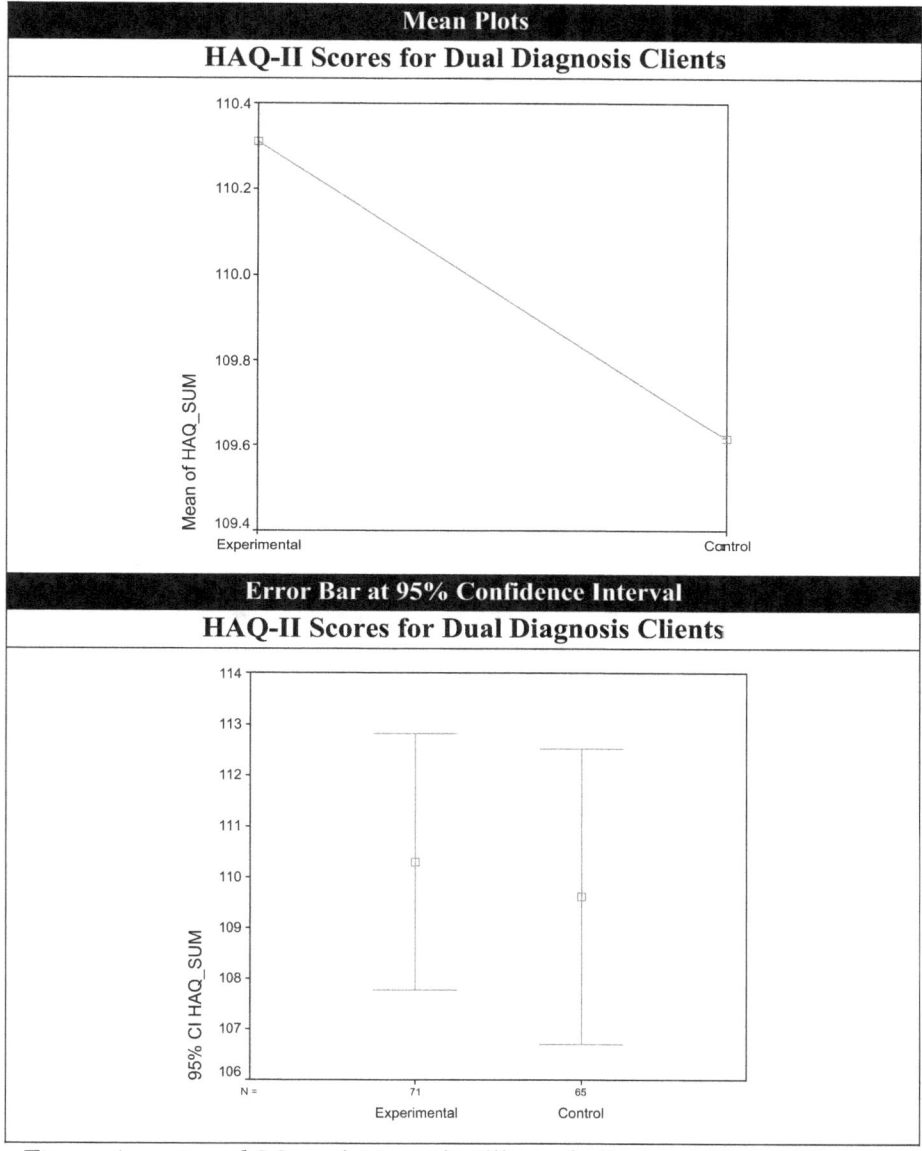

Figure 4 continued. Mean therapeutic alliance indicators in the AAT group (n = 135) and the control group (n = 96) separated into by specific subgroups. The difference was not statistically significant for dual diagnosis clients $F(1, 134)$ .130, $p > .719$.

Figure continued

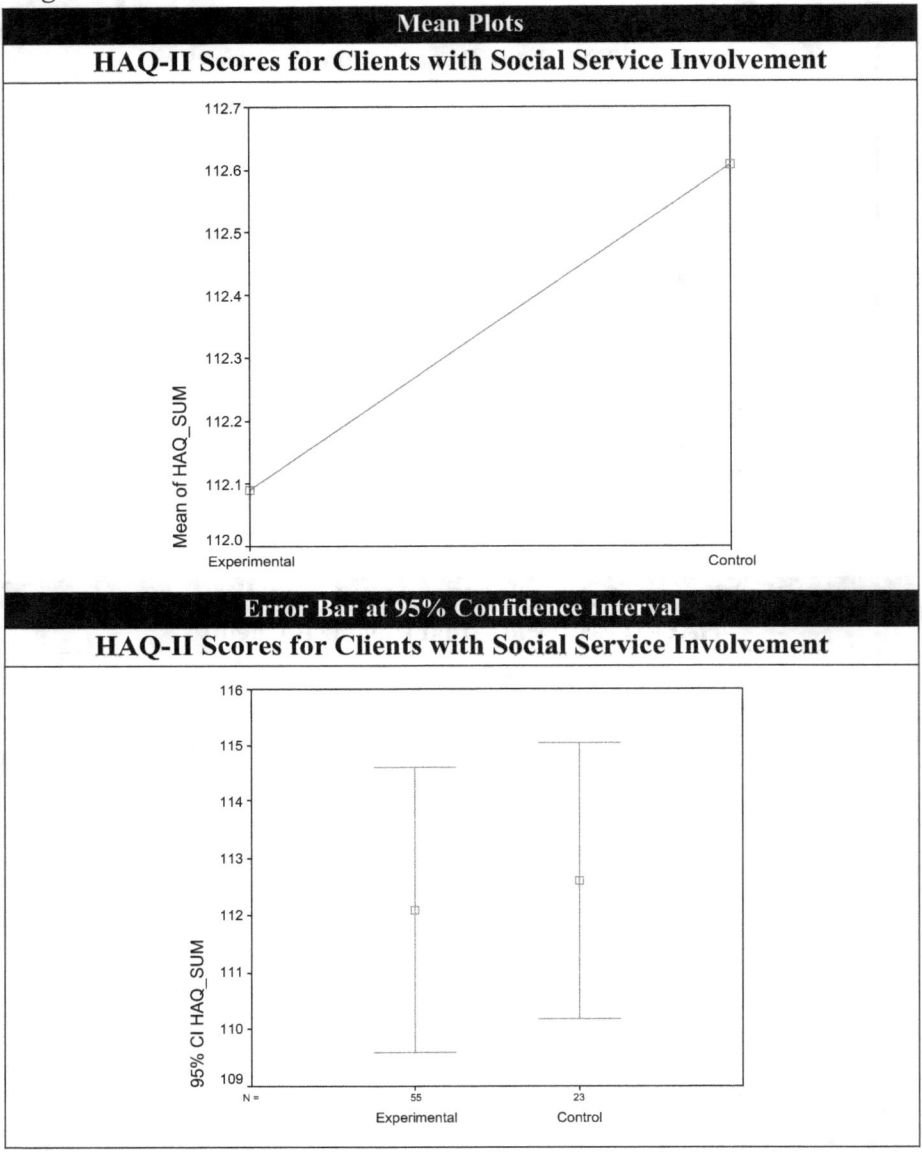

Figure 4 continued. Mean therapeutic alliance indicators in the AAT group (n = 135) and the control group (n = 96) separated into by specific subgroups. The difference was not statistically significant for clients with social service involvement $F(1, 76)$ .062, $p > .804$.

Figure continued

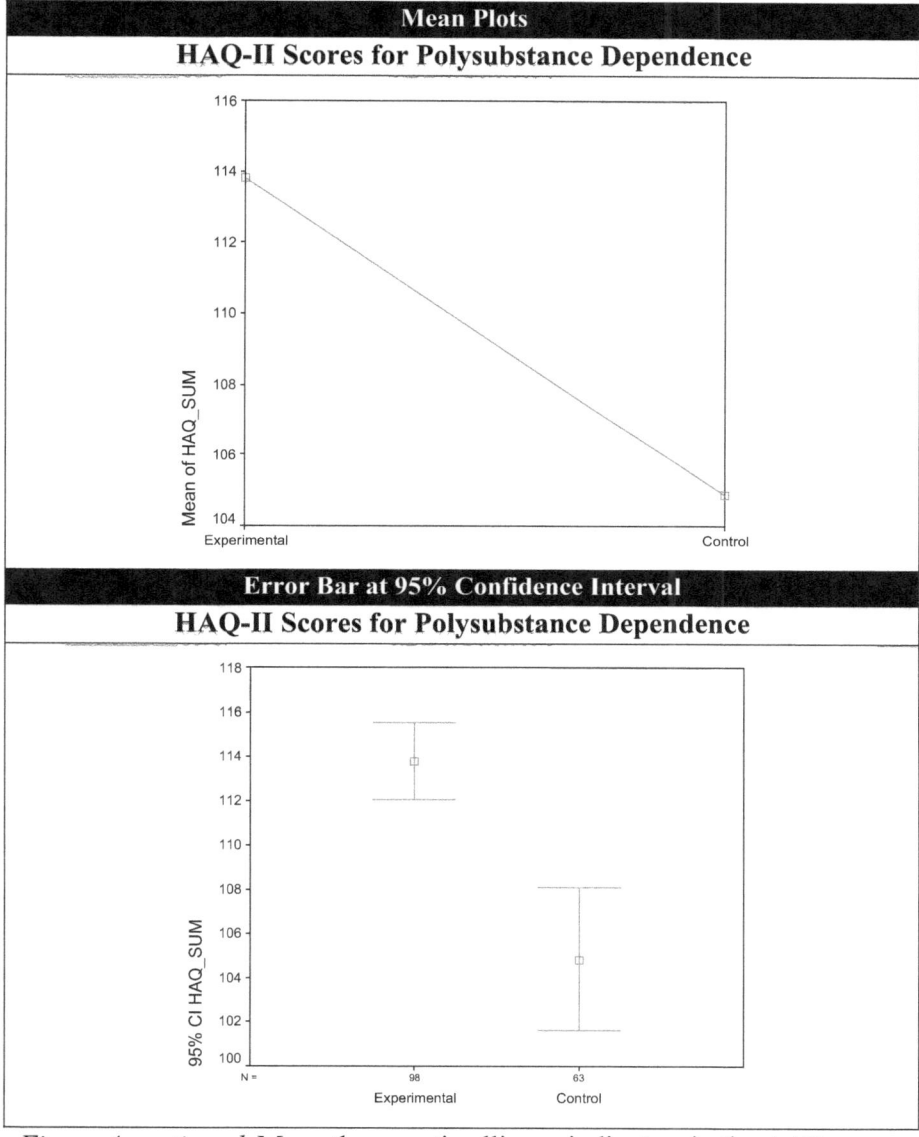

Figure 4 continued. Mean therapeutic alliance indicators in the AAT group (n = 135) and the control group (n = 96) separated by specific subgroups. The AAT group had higher alliance rates for polysubstance dependent clients $F(1, 159)$ 27.85, $p < .000$.

Figure continued

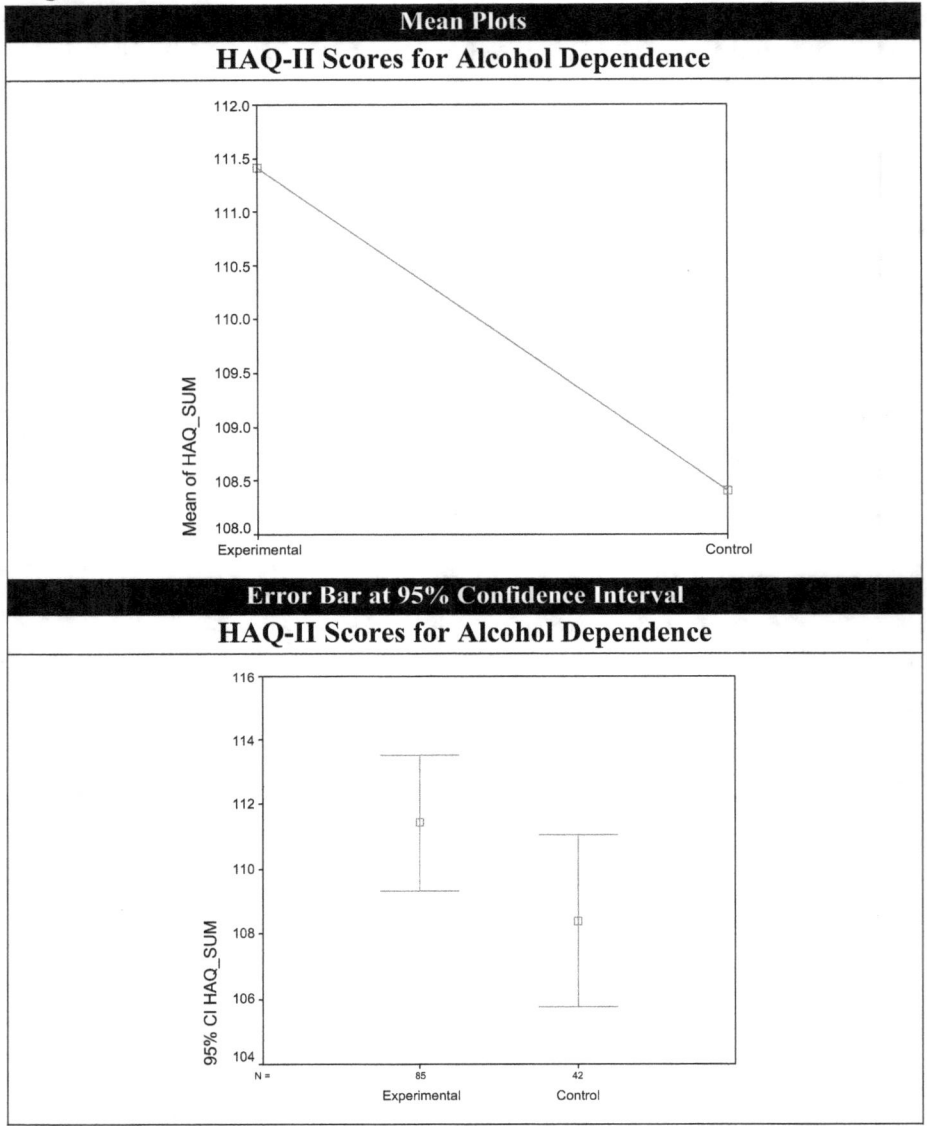

Figure 4 continued. Mean therapeutic alliance indicators in the AAT group (n = 135) and the control group (n = 96) separated by specific subgroups. The AAT group had higher alliance rates for cannabis dependent clients $F(1, 112)$ 24.96, $p < .000$.

Figure continued

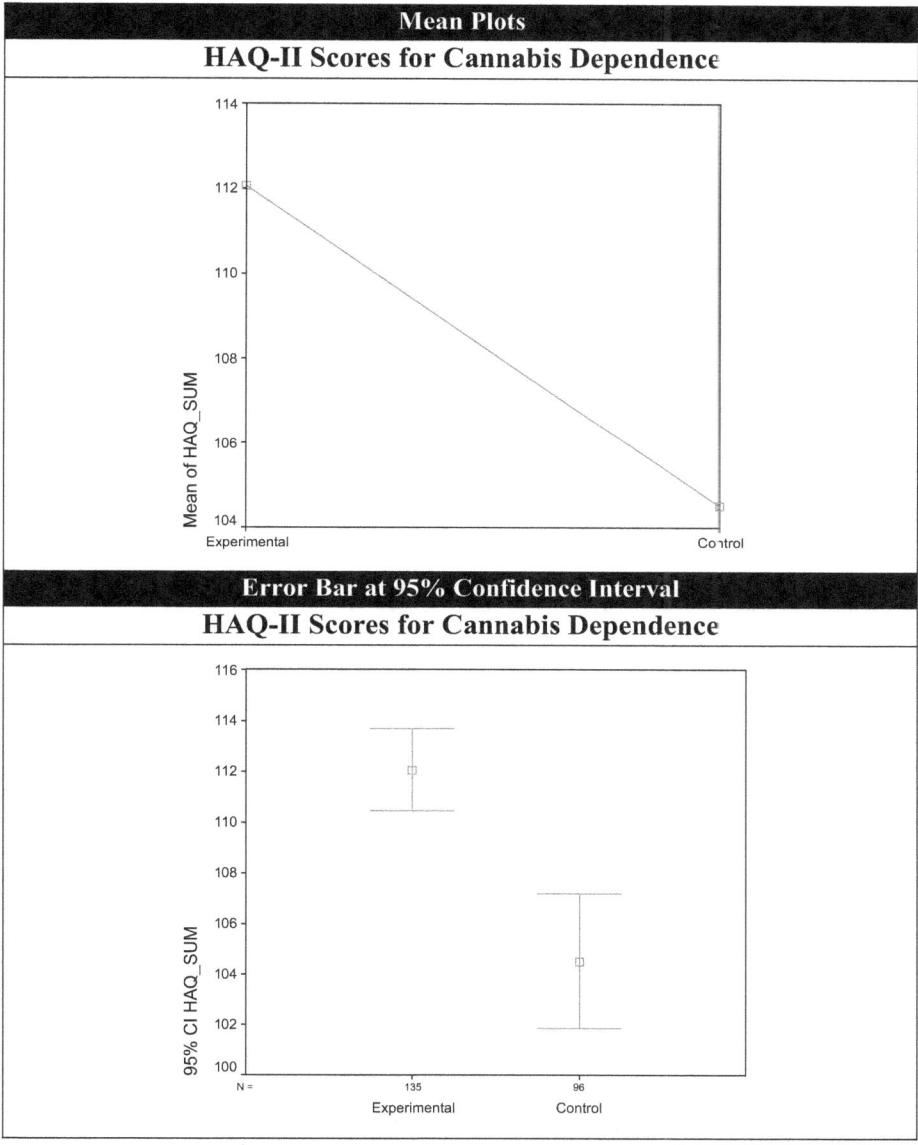

Figure 4 continued. Mean therapeutic alliance indicators in the AAT group (n = 135) and the control group (n = 96) separated by specific subgroups. The difference was not statistically significant for alcohol dependent clients $F(1, 125)$ 2.91, $p > .091$.

Figure continued

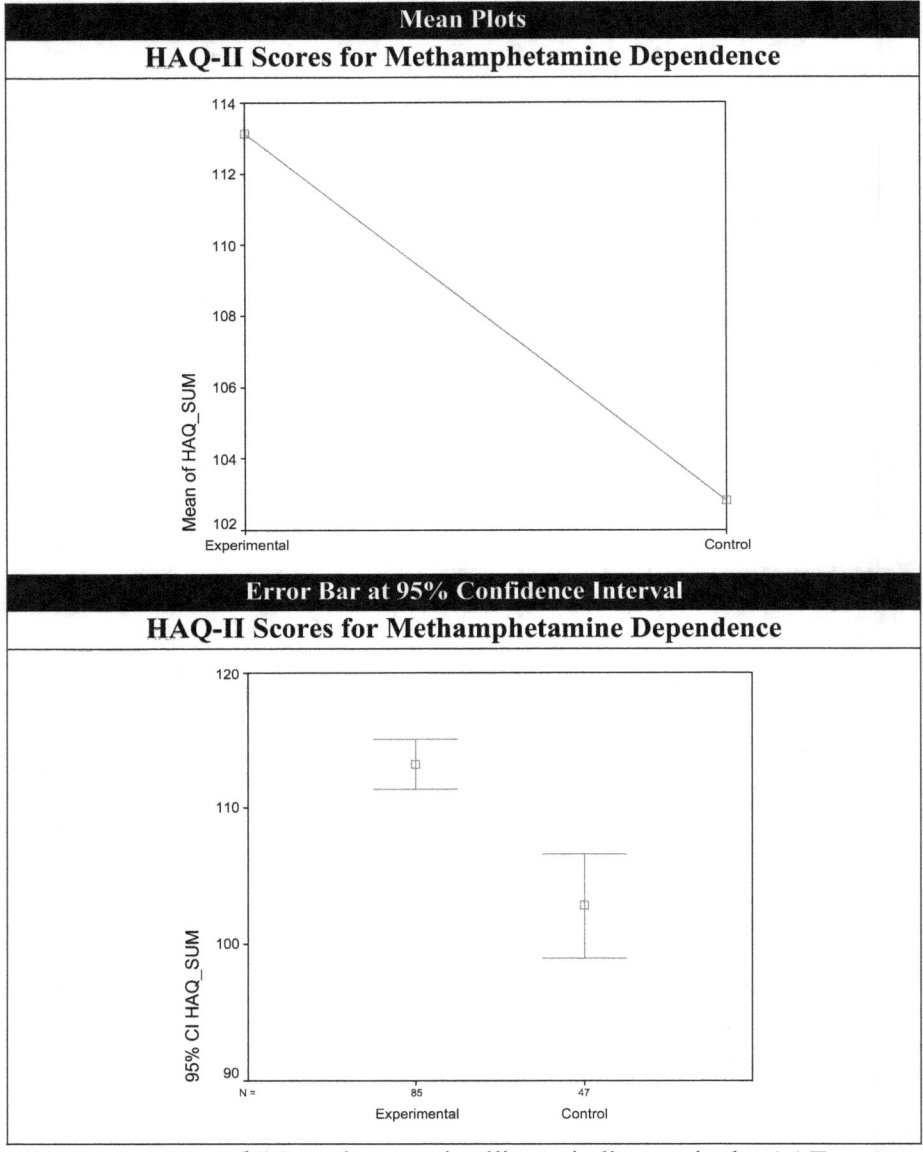

Figure 4 continued. Mean therapeutic alliance indicators in the AAT group (n = 135) and the control group (n = 96) separated by specific subgroups. The AAT experimental group had higher alliance rates for methamphetamine dependent clients $F(1, 130)$ 29.57, $p < .000$.

Summary

The population characteristics appear to be alike for most categories between both groups. Highlights indicate there were equal levels of gender represented for both groups and equal representation of ethnic differences. A large portion of the participants was seeking treatment for more than one substance and for a dual diagnosis.

The results indicate significant differences between clients in AAT groups and control groups for three of the four dependent variables assessed. The results of the HAQ-II data confirm the hypotheses that the therapeutic alliance is strengthened with the addition of a therapy dog in a residential substance abuse treatment center providing services to substance dependent adult clients. In the case of heart rates and diastolic blood pressure rates, clients in the AAT groups experienced greater decreases in their vital signs than those in the groups that did not utilize AAT. A review of the effect sizes calculated for each variable suggests that the addition of AAT therapy contributed most to the differences observed for mean HAQ-II ratings and the vital sign statistics.

Finally, various demographic subgroups were assessed from the participating population. The results were mixed. Clients seeking treatment for a dual diagnosis, with social service involvement in their life or seeking treatment for alcohol were not found to have significant results between groups. However, females, males, court ordered clients, pet owners, and clients seeking treatment for polysubstance use, cannabis and methamphetamines indicated that the therapeutic alliance was strengthened with the addition of a therapy dog to the group session.

The next chapter will discuss and interpret the findings of this study. It will further discuss the social significance of the study and make recommendations for future research.

CHAPTER 5
CONCLUSIONS AND RECOMMENDATIONS

Introduction

In the last chapter, the results verify the hypothesis that AAT would strengthen the therapeutic alliance with adult clients seeking treatment for substance dependence. A review of the effect sizes calculated for the variable suggests that the addition of AAT therapy contributed most to the differences observed for mean HAQ-II ratings. Additionally, two of the three dependent variables for the second hypothesis were also verified. AAT was found to increase HAQ-II scores and decrease both the heart rate and diastolic blood pressure. Although AAT did reduce systolic blood pressure rates, the findings were not significant. Many population subgroups were also assessed with mixed results. The results indicate that AAT did increase the therapeutic alliance between the client and therapist and helped to reduce indicators of stress in group therapy. In this chapter, the findings will be explored and expanded. Implications for social change and recommendations will also be discussed.

Interpretation and Discussion of the Findings

The results of this research project help to verify and support the theoretical foundations for this study including social support theory. The clients participating in AAT developed a therapeutic relationship with the therapist leading to the development of bonds of mutual trust, acceptance, and confidence in others. AAT contributed to the individual reaching out and placing trust in another human being. This simple bond is foundational for the client to connect with other social support systems. The enhancement of the therapeutic alliance with AAT requires reciprocity, mutuality and social exchange (Antonucci, 1985).

The results of this study also supported attachment theory and its application to AAT with substance abuse treatment. AAT helped reinforce the attachment between the therapist and the client. The therapeutic alliance and the therapy animal worked as a temporary surrogate of attachment so that other support attachments can be learned and attained. AAT helped to strengthen the therapeutic alliance, which can strengthen the potential for supportive future secure attachments. A strong therapeutic alliance also can teach the client appropriate interdependence, communication skills, mutual respect, trust and caring that can be transferred to future relationships.

AAT increased the measures of the therapeutic alliance. Increasing the therapeutic alliance can significantly improve the probability of recovery success for clients seeking treatment for substance dependence. The quality of the alliance and not the technique or theory is most predictive of recovery outcome success. A client receiving AAT is more likely to benefit from the treatment process, higher retention rates and less frequent episodes of drug and alcohol relapse (Meier, Donmall, McElduff, Barrowclough, & Heller, 2006).

One reason for this increase in the therapeutic alliance could be the perception from the clients that the therapist was more caring and could be trusted more than someone who did not own or love animals. However, in this study the control group clients were aware of the therapist's love of animals and could have seen the therapy dog enter or exit the facility when doing therapy for the experimental group. This suggests that the control group may have increased measures in the therapeutic alliance and reduced stress levels simply with this knowledge. Therefore, the results could potentially have been even greater between groups if the therapist would have conducted the control group and the experimental group at different facilities. Unfortunately, this change would bring in additional variables that would need to be assessed.

Psychological stress can contribute to drug and alcohol relapse (Brandy & Sonne, 1999). This study suggests that AAT decreases stress through the decrease in heart rates and diastolic blood pressure rates. With reduced psychological stress, clients are freer to express themselves verbally in a group setting (Yalom, 2005). With this decrease and an increase in the measures of the therapeutic alliance, clients exposed to AAT seem to have a better chance of treatment success than the traditional control group. The therapy animal seems to help clients overcome the depression and anxiety often associated with being in residential treatment, especially those who are court ordered or came to the residential treatment setting from jail or prison (Bardill & Hutchinson, 1997; Campbell-Berg, 2000). A person coping with the stress of compulsory residential or inpatient treatment may feel like his or her world is tumbling down around them, yet the therapy animal remained constant. The evidence suggests that AAT added to a therapeutic milieu can enhance motivation, encouragement, inspiration, and insight into the therapeutic process. AAT improves retention and motivation for participation in therapy (Holcomb & Meacham, 1989).

In this study, the systolic blood pressure was reduced but not significantly, as was the diastolic blood pressure rate and heart rate with AAT. The reason for this phenomenon is unknown.

Traditionally the diastolic blood pressure has been the most important component of blood pressure but in recent years, the systolic pressure rate has been found to be a better predictor of risk, at least for hypertension among aging adults (Strandberg, 2003).

The results of the data analysis of the population subgroups were diverse. The study indicated that AAT is a viable complementary therapy for both male and female clients. It is a viable option for clients seeking treatment for polysubstance dependence, cannabis dependence and methamphetamine dependence. Additionally AAT is a viable option for clients who are court ordered into treatment or clients who own or have recently owned pets of their own. Positive results can be found with only one session.

AAT was very effective in increasing the therapeutic alliance for clients seeking treatment for an addiction to illegal drugs and for clients who were court ordered for treatment. These clients are most likely to come to treatment under the worst of circumstances. Many have been living in shelters, on the streets or coming directly from jail or prison. Nearly all have felony convictions with charges pending. These clients have not had the comforts of home for some time. The therapy animal could be seen as a novelty to the therapeutic process. It could also remind the client of better days and give the client a since of home and normalcy.

AAT was not found to be as effective for clients seeking treatment for a dual diagnosis, clients who were being investigated by the state social service department (child protective services) and clients seeking treatment for alcohol. The clients seeking treatment for alcohol reported that AAT did improve the therapeutic alliance but the results were not significant. This study indicated that AAT was a viable option for clients seeking treatment for methamphetamine, cannabis and polysubstance dependence. Since drug dependent clients and alcohol dependent clients usually represent different age groups, the difference in statistical significance may be explained for by age characteristics. For example, methamphetamine dependent clients are usually younger in age while alcohol dependent clients tend to be more mature. Another potential explanation for the difference could be the legality of the substance. Clients coming to treatment for methamphetamine, cannabis or polysubstance dependency are usually court ordered with felony charges pending. Clients seeking treatment for alcohol dependence have been using a legal drug for years and are more likely to come to treatment due to relationship, family or health reasons. Clients with alcohol dependency are more likely to have come to treatment from their home environment while clients seeking treatment for illicit drugs are more likely to come from jail and may not have enjoyed the comforts of home for years. The alcohol dependent client is more prone to have a pet at home and not be as impressed with the novelty of the therapy dog at the treatment center as deeply as others those who have not had these freedoms.

Dual diagnosis clients and clients involved with social services did not appear to benefit from one session of AAT in a group setting. The reason for this phenomenon is unknown. It is possible that having more than one session of AAT could have improved ratings of the therapeutic alliance. Clients with a dual diagnosis and clients with social service or child protective service involvement may require multiple sessions to test the hypothesis due to various potential variables.

The development of a therapeutic alliance with a client with a substance abuse disorder and a mental health disorder can be challenging for both the client and the therapist. Many therapists feel comfortable in their expertise of either mental health or addictions but rarely does a therapist welcome the combination. These clients can be a challenge and require special helping professionals with the time it takes for these individuals to change. These clients also often experience demoralization and despair due to the complexity of these two unique and challenging problems. Inspiring hope is often a necessary precursor to a fully established therapeutic alliance. This requires additional time to the process. This study into the effectiveness AAT was not designed for this timeframe. Clients with a co-occurring disorder may require additional sessions before the benefits of AAT of lack thereof are truly realized.

Clients with state social service involvement indicate that they are being investigated by child protective services for child neglect, child abuse, or child abandonment. A majority of these clients had their children removed from their home and they have come to residential treatment as one requirement to get their children back. This group is usually consisting of young uneducated women living in poverty and overwhelmed with life, love and the complexity of the social service system. Over 80 percent of substantiated cases of child abuse and neglect involve substance abuse and poverty (SAMHSA, 2000). They are also struggling with the stigma of being labeled both an addict and bad parent; or even worse, a child abuser. They are struggling themselves to understand why they would continue to abuse drugs and alcohol at the expense of their own children.

Many times, these clients have also been victims themselves. Research suggests that many were victims of abuse and neglect when they were children (SAMHSA, 2000). Additionally, many of these clients have been betrayed by lovers, family members and have perceptions of betrayal by their state workers and other professionals. This perception often leads to severe defensiveness in the treatment environment. They are often afraid to open up verbally because they could bring up issues that could be used against them later as evidence to sever their parental rights. With present state and federal laws, these concerns are somewhat valid. They seem not to have the same protections as other clients when opening up emotionally and verbally in a group setting.

This condition creates a very complex dilemma for the client and the therapist alike. If the client does not open up about their drug use and consequences with their children, they are often seen as resistant and become in danger of being discharged prematurely from their required treatment. However, if they do disclose openly and the information is forwarded to the child abuse investigator, this discloser could strengthen the child welfare case against her. The therapist continues to work toward a strong therapeutic alliance but the client's resistance is difficult to overcome. This study into the effectiveness AAT was not designed for the time and techniques necessary to develop a strong therapeutic alliance with this specialized group. Clients with a social service involvement may require additional sessions before the benefits of AAT, or lack thereof, are truly realized.

Recommendations and Implications for Social Change

In 2003, there were 1.84 million individual substance abuse treatment admissions (SAMHSA, 2006a). In the same year, 28% of clients in treatment left against professional advice and an additional 9% were terminated by the facility. Only 44% successfully completed treatment (SAMHSA, 2006b). Since treatment for alcohol and drug dependence are not very effective (Cuttler & Fishbain, 2005), new treatment strategies are needed to help with client retention in treatment and increase treatment efficacy. The greatest predictor of treatment success is the quality of the therapeutic relationship (Orlinsky, Ronnestad, & Wilutzki, 2003). This study shows that AAT significantly improved the quality of the therapeutic relationship, which may result in higher treatment outcomes and reduced physiological indicators of psychological stress. This study has the potential to promote significant social change on treatment programs throughout the world. Residential treatment centers, and potentially outpatient treatment programs, can improve treatment outcome by an improved therapeutic alliance with a trained therapy dog present in group treatment. AAT can reduce stress and improve retention and motivation for participation in therapy resulting in an increase in recovery success. The research findings indicate that AAT should be a serious consideration for nearly every addiction treatment center. Even for the population subgroups that did not appear to benefit from AAT, they were not harmed by the practice either. The AAT experience for these select groups simply did not make a difference. Therefore, to receive the maximum benefits for most clients, AAT should be added to several addiction treatment programs to increase the therapeutic alliance, recovery outcome and decrease psychological stress experienced by many who enter the program.

This study may also prove to be a foundational study for additional research in the field that was suggested by Fine (2006) in his authoritative work on AAT. He suggested that "the gold standard for research of this type is to have a random assignment to an AAT format and a traditional therapy format and then to determine which format led to a better therapeutic outcome" (Fine & Mio, p. 517). This quantitative study followed these recommendations by using randomized populations and controlled conditions to establish the effects of chosen variables that influence the therapeutic alliance and therapeutic outcome.

Recommendations for Action

This researcher is scheduled to conduct various state and local workshops for the Kentucky Counseling Association in the fall of 2006 and the annual conference in Detroit for the American Counseling Association in the spring of 2007. These workshops will review the results of this study and demonstrate the benefits of AAT with the participants utilizing the therapy dog used in this project. Journal articles are being written from the results of this study and will be submitted in 2007. Given the upcoming publication of this dissertation and having the portions of the material published in peer review journals, the results should be adequately disseminated to the scientific community.

This researcher will be seeking a full-time appointment as an associate professor at a local college or university where he is currently teaching on an adjunct basis. This appointment will also lend this researcher opportunity to disseminate the research findings to new students, educational colleagues and professionals in the field of counseling and addiction. Once the findings are adequately published in the scientific literature, article submissions will be made to addiction professional trade magazines and magazines that would interest the pet enthusiast. These articles will point to the research findings published in the peer review literature.

The American public may also find the results of this study fascinating. A large majority of the population own pet animals and may find the study results supporting their own strongly held beliefs. The American public has been severely impacted by addictions, in one form or another, and may find the results educational, helping them to make wiser decisions when deciding on a treatment program for themselves or a loved one. Considering the results of this study could help individuals to choose one program incorporating AAT over another treatment program that does not have this empirically sound complementary alternative. It should also be noted that the results of this study could fancy the news service due to its potential interest to the public. This would allow excerpts of the study results to be published in newspapers throughout the world.

Recommendations for Future Research

The findings in this study can serve as a foundation for future studies. Since AAT was found to be a successful treatment by enhancing the therapeutic relationship, future studies can help to determine why and how this happens. Additional empirical studies are needed along with good qualitative studies to enhance the empirical findings.

It is recommended that assessment continue to show the ongoing validity of AAT in a substance abuse treatment facility. This study showed how AAT was successful in a group setting but individual substance abuse treatment may prove to be even more successful. This study also focused on the adult population in residential treatment. It would be recommended to expand the population for research purposes to include adolescents and outpatient settings. Clients may also find additional success if matched with high PAS scores. Further research is needed to determine a correlation between high PAS scores and scores of perceived therapeutic alliance.

The assessment of specific population subgroups in the addiction field need to be further explored. This study answered specific questions but it also raised additional ones. Studies should further explore the efficacy of AAT with clients with a dual diagnosis and clients with social service involvement. It is also recommended to explore the questions raised above concerning the difference seen in clients seeking treatment for illicit drugs and a legal drug, alcohol. With the tremendous increase in methamphetamine abuse and dependency in the country, it is important to develop therapies to counter this increase. This study indicated that AAT was a viable option for clients seeking treatment for methamphetamine dependency. It is recommended that additional studies be conducted to determine the efficacy of this population due to the almost epidemic need. Studies that look at specific chemical dependencies should account for other variables such as client age, legal history and social support.

More research is needed to determine if the diastolic blood pressure is indeed the only component of blood pressure influenced by AAT or whether these measures are influenced by conditions unrelated to this study. Other research studies seem to indicate that both diastolic and systolic measures are reduced with the addition of AAT (Baun, Bergastrom, Langston, & Thoma, 1984; Nagengast, Baun, Megel, & Leibowitz, 1997).

In this study, vital signs were taken prior to the beginning of the group session and were collected after the group session. Only one paraprofessional staff member measured these vital signs taking several minutes for each group session. This created a situation in which individuals were waiting in line to have their vital signs read. For substance abuse clients who have a tremendous desire to go outside to smoke cigarettes after a one hour group session, waiting in line was very difficult for them and may have raised their stress levels and readings slightly. It is recommended that standardized procedures for vital sign collection be addressed. Standards should address the following questions:

1.   How quickly should the vital signs be taken after the treatment? The longer the delay in the vital signs being taken the more intervening variables could interfere with the readings. If vital signs should be taken within 5 minutes before and 5 minutes after the sessions then additional medical technicians should be procured to be available to collect the data in a more timely fashion. However, increasing the number of technicians may also bring additional variables that may influence the outcome.

2.   Should the participants move from the group to the station where vitals will be taken or should the medical technicians come to the room where the participants received their treatment? It is possible that the action of physical movement to a nurses' station and standing in line to be measured for vital signs could introduce additional intervening variables to the study.

3.   Is there a difference in vital sign rate reduction for those who smoke cigarettes and habitually smoke after each session and those who do not smoke? This researcher has observed for many years in doing substance abuse therapy groups that clients who smoke cigarettes become very anxious toward the end of any group session. Smokers could increase their heart rate and blood pressure rates due to their habituated association with smoking on the hour and after a scheduled group session. Because of this, smoker vital sign rates could be significantly different from their nonsmoking peers.

4.   Is there a difference in vital sign rates for the first group in the morning compared to the next group, which is closer to a mealtime? Timing could be a significant variable that was not seriously considered in this project. It is recommended that standards be developed that address timing for vital sign collection in a group setting.

The results of the analysis of the population subgroups also raised additional questions and the need for additional research. It is recommended that AAT be tested further for clients with a dual diagnosis because the results of this study seem to contradict additional studies indicating that clients with a mental health disorder do benefit from AAT (Hooker, Freeman, & Stewart, 2002). Clients with children removed by child protective services or being investigated by child protective services also appeared not to benefit from one session of AAT. This phenomenon needs to be further explored. This specific population appears to be particularly suspicious of treatment professionals and may need additional time to develop a therapeutic alliance regardless of whether AAT was part of the intervention. It is recommended that additional studies look into increasing the amount of group sessions with this and other populations.

Conclusion

The purpose of this study was to evaluate the relationship of Animal Assisted Therapy (AAT) on the therapeutic alliance with an adult residential substance abuse population in group therapy. This quantitative study included an experimental design using a randomized population and controlled conditions to establish the effects of the chosen variables that influence outcome. This study hypothesizes that clients in an AAT group session would show higher ratings of the therapeutic alliance, as measured on the Helping Alliance Questionnaire (HAQ-II), over clients in a group therapy session without the therapy dog present. This research also hypothesizes that clients in an AAT group session will demonstrate lowered stress levels, as measured by lowered blood pressure (diastolic and systolic) and heart rate over clients in a group therapy session without the therapy dog present.

AAT was found to increase HAQ-II scores and decrease both the heart rate and diastolic blood pressure. AAT did reduce systolic blood pressure rates but the findings were not significant. This finding confirmed the hypothesis that the experimental group with the therapy dog would result in significantly higher ratings of a positive therapeutic alliance than the control group without the therapy dog present. The results indicate that the therapeutic alliance is enhanced with the addition of a therapy dog within a group setting with adult clients in a residential drug abuse treatment setting. Additionally, the findings for both the heart rate and diastolic blood pressure partly confirmed the hypothesis that the experimental group with the therapy dog would result in significantly lower scores than the control group without the therapy dog present. The results revealed that two of three indicators of reduced stress levels are significantly lowered with the addition of a therapy dog within a group setting with adult clients in a residential drug abuse treatment setting.

Population subgroups were assessed with mixed results. Clients seeking treatment for a dual diagnosis, clients with state social service involvement and clients seeking treatment for alcohol did not verify the efficacy for AAT. The population subgroups of males, females, pet owners, court ordered clients, and clients seeking treatment for polysubstance dependence, cannabis dependence and methamphetamine dependence all supported the hypothesis and verified the efficacy for AAT.

Finally, the results of the study were explored and interpreted. The study has significant implications for social change for the substance abuse treatment industry. A call for empirical research was recently posed by Fine and Mio (2006). In their call for additional research, they suggested that "the gold standard for research of this type is to have a random assignment to an AAT format and a traditional therapy format and then to determine which format led to a better therapeutic outcome" (Fine & Mio, p. 517). This quantitative study followed these recommendations by using randomized populations and controlled conditions to establish the effects of chosen variables that influence outcome. This study can be used as an empirically sound foundational study for the efficacy of AAT with a substance abuse population and for the enhancement of the therapeutic alliance in a group treatment environment. Limitations of the study were explored and recommendations for additional research were given. Specifically, future AAT research testing blood pressure and heart rate differences need to have standardized procedures to assure consistency in reducing intervening variables for the study need to be established.

REFERENCES

Ader, R. (2006). *Psychoneuroimmunology* (4th ed.). New York: Academic Press.

Ainsworth, M. (1989). Attachment beyond infancy. *American Psychologist, 44,* 709-716.

Ainsworth, M. D. S. (1967). *Infancy in Uganda: Infant care and the growth of attachment.* Baltimore, MD: Johns Hopkins University Press.

Ainsworth, M. D., Blehar, M. C., Waters, E., & Wall, S. (1978). *Patterns of attachment: A psychological study of the strange situation.* Hillsdale, NJ: Erlbaum.

Albrecht, T., & Adelman, M. (1987). Communication networks as structures of social support. In T. Alcrecht & M. Adelman (Eds.), *Communicating social support* (pp. 40-61). Newbury Park, CA: Sage.

Allen, C. L. (1989, February). The success of authority in prison management. *Insights on the news,* 8-19.

Allen, K. (2003). Are pets a healthy pleasure? The influence of pets on blood pressure. *Current Directions in Psychological Science, 12*(6), 236-239.

Allen, K. M., Blascovich, J., Tomaka, K., & Kelsey, R. M. (2001). Presence of human friends and pet dogs as moderators of autonomic responses to stress in women. *Journal of Personality and Social Psychology, 61,* 582-589.

Allen, K., Shykoff, B. E., & Izzo, J. L., Jr. (2001). Pet ownership but not ACE inhibitor therapy blunts home blood pressure responses to mental stress. *Hypertension, 38,* 815-820.

Allen, K.; Blascovich, J.; Mendes, W. B. (2002). Cardiovascular reactivity in the presence of pets, friends, and spouses: The truth about cats and dogs. *Psychosomatic Medicine, 64, 727-739.*

Altschuler, E. L. (1999). Pet-facilitated therapy for posttraumatic stress disorder. *Annals of Clinical Psychiatry, 11*(1), 29-30.

American Pet Products Manufacturers Association (2005, March). *2005/2006 APPMA National Pet Owners Survey.* Washington DC: APPMA.

American Psychiatric Association (2000). *Diagnostic and statistical manual of mental disorders-TR* (4th ed.). Washington, DC: Author.

American Society of Addiction Medicine, Inc. (2001). *ASAM Patient placement criteria for the treatment of substance-related disorders* (2nd ed., Rev.). Chevy Chase, MD: American Society of Addiction Medicine, Inc.

Anderson, W. P., Reid, C. M., & Jennings, G. L. (1992). Pet ownership and risk factors for cardiovascular disease. *Medical Journal of Australia, 157,* 298-301.

Antonucci, T. C. (1985). Social support: theoretical advances, recent findings and pressing issues. In I. G. Sarason & B. R. Sarason (Eds.), *Social support: theory, research and application* (pp. 21-37). Boston: Nijhoff Publishers.

Antonucci, T. C., & Jackson, J. S. (1990). The role of reciprocity in social support. In B. R. Sarason, I. G. Sarason & G. R. Pierce (Eds.), *Social support: An interactional view* (pp. 173-209). New York: Wiley.

Arkow, P. (2000). Synergy and symbiosis in animal-assisted therapy: Interdisciplinary collaborations. In A.H. Fine (Ed.), *Handbook of animal-assisted therapy* (pp. 433-448). San Diego, CA: Academic Press.

Arkrow, P. (1993). *Pet-Therapy: A study and resource guide the use of companion animals in selected therapies.* Colorado Springs, CO: The Humane Society of the Pikes Peak Region.

Ascione, F. R. (1992). Enhancing children's attitudes about the humane treatment of animals: Generalization to human-directed empathy. *Anthrozoos, 5*(3), 176-191.

Auerbach, S. M. (1989). Stress management and coping research in the health care setting: A review and methodological commentary. *Journal of Consulting and Clinical Psychology, 57,* 388-395.

Bachelor, A. (1991). Comparison and relationship to outcome of diverse dimensions of the helping alliance as seen by client and therapist. *Psychotherapy, 28*(3), 534-549.

Bachelor, A., & Horvath, A. (1999). The therapeutic relationship. In M. A. Hubble, B. L. Duncan, and S. D. Miller (Ed.), *The heart and soul of change: What works in therapy* (pp. 133-178). Washington D. C.: APA Press.

Barak, Y., Savorai, O., Mavashev, S., & Beni, A. (2001). Animal assisted therapy for elderly schizophrenic patients: A one year controlled trial. *American Journal of Geriatric Psychiatry, 9*(4), 439-432.

Barba, B. E. (1995). A critical review of the research on the human/companion animal relationship: 1988-1993. *Anthrozoos, 8*(1), 9-14.

Bardill, N., & Hutchinson, S. (1997). Animal-assisted therapy with hospitalized adolescents. *Journal of Child and Adolescent Psychiatric Nursing, 10*(1), 17-24.

Barker, S. B., & Dawson, K. S. (1998). The effects of animal-assisted therapy on anxiety ratings of hospitalized psychiatric patients. *Psychiatric Services, 49,* 797-801.

Barker, S. B., Best, A. M., Fredrickson, M., & Hunter, G. (2000). Constraints in assessing the impact of animals in education. *Anthrozoos, 13*(2), 74-79.

Bartholomew, K., & Horowitz, L. M. (1991). Attachment styles among young adults: A test of a four-category model. *Journal of Personality and Social Change, 61,* 226-244.

Batson, K., McCabe, B., Baun, M. M., & Wilson, C. (1997). The effect of a therapy dog on socialization and physiological indicators of stress in persons diagnosed with Alzheimer's disease. In C.C. Wilson & D.C. Turner (Eds.), *Companion animals in human health* (pp. 203-215). London: Sage.

Baumeister, R. F., & Leary, M. R. (1995). The need to belong: Desire for interpersonal attachments as a fundamental human motivation. *Psychological Bulletin, 117,* 497-529.

Baun, M. M., & McCabe, B. W. (2003). Companion animals and persons with dementia of the Alzheimer's type. *American Behavioralist Scientist, 47*(1), 42-51.

Baun, M., Bergastrom, N., Langston, N., & Thoma, L. (1984). Physiological effects of human/companion animal bonding. *Nursing Research, 15,* 126-129.

Beck, A. M. (2000). The use of animals to benefit humans, animal-assisted therapy. In A.H. Fine (Ed.), *The handbook on animal-assisted therapy: Theoretical foundations and guidelines for practice* (pp. 21-40). San Diego, CA: Academic Press.

Beck, A. M., & Katcher, A. H. (2003). Future directions in human-animal bond research. *American Behavioral Scientist, 47*(1), 79-93.

Beck, A. M., Seraydarian, I., & Hunter, G. F. (1986). The use of animals in the rehabilitation of psychiatric inpatients. *Psychological Reports, 8,* 63-66.

Beck, A. T., Wright, F. D., Newman, C. F., & Liese, B. S. (1993). *Cognitive therapy of substance abuse*. New York: Guilford Press.

Beck, A., & Katcher, A. (1983). *Between pets and people: The importance of animal companionship*. New York: G. P. Putnam's Sons.

Beck, A., & Katcher, A. (1996). *Between pets and people: The importance of animal companionship*. West Lafayette, IN: Purdue University Press.

Becker, M. (2002). *The healing power of pets*. New York: Hyperion.

Bissell, L., & Royce, J. E. (1987). *Ethics for Addiction Professionals* (2nd ed.). Center City, MN: Hazelden.

Blatt, S. J., Zuroff, D. C., Quinlan, D. M., & Pilkonis, P. (1996). Interpersonal factors in brief treatment of depression: Further analyses of data from the NIMH Treatment of Depression Collaborative Research Program. *Journal of Consulting and Clinical Psychology, 64,* 1276-1284.

Bonas, S., McNicholas, J., & Collis, G. M. (2000). Pets in the network of family relationships: An empirical study. In A. Podberscek, E. Paul & J. Serpell (Eds.), *Companion animals and us: Exploring the relationships between people and pets* (pp. 209-236). New York: Cambridge University Press.

Bordin, E. S. (1979). The generalizabilily of the psychoanalytic concept of the working alliance. *Psychotherapy: Theory, Research, and Practice, 6,* 252-260.

Bossard, J. (1944). The mental hygiene of owning a dog. *Mental Hygiene, 24,* 408-413

Bowlby, J. (1969). *Attachment and loss: Attachment* (Vol. 1). New York: Basic.

Bowlby, J. (1988). *A secure base. Clinical applications of attachment theory.* London: Routledge.

Braaten, L. J. (1990). The difference patterns of group climate critical incidents in high and low cohesion sessions of group psychotherapy. *International Journal of Group Psychotherapy, 40,* 477-493.

Brady, K. T., & Sonne, S. C. (1999). The role of stress in alcohol use, alcoholism treatment, and relapse. *Alcohol Research & Health, 23*(4), 263-271.

Brasic, J. R. (1998). Pets and health. *Psychological Reports, 83,* 1011-1024.

Brennan, P. L., Moos, R. H., & Kelly, K. M. (1994). Spouses of late-life problem drinkers: Functioning coping responses, and family contexts. *Journal of Family Psychology, 8,* 447-457.

Bretherton, I., & Munholland, K. A. (1999). Internal working models in attachment relationships. In J. Cassidy & P. R. Saver (Eds.), *Handbook of attachment: Theory, research, and clinical applications* (pp. 89-111). New York: Guilford.

Brickel, C. M. (1986). Pet-facilitated therapies: A review of the literature and clinical implementation considerations. *Clinical Gerontologist, 5,* 309-332.

Briggs, D. B. (2006). Therapist stress, career sustaining behavior, coping and the working alliance (Doctoral dissertation, Western Michigan University, 2006). *Dissertation Abstracts International, AA13183585.*

Brodie, S. J., & Biley, F. C. (1999). An exploration of the potential benefits of pet-facilitated therapy. *Journal of Clinical Nursing, 8,* 329-337.

Brodie, S. J., Biley, F. C., & Shewring, M. (2002). An exploration of the potential risks associated with using pet therapy in healthcare settings. *Journal of Clinical Nursing, 11,* 444-456.

Brook, D. W., & Spitz, H. I. (2002). *group therapy of substance abuse*. Binghamton, NY: Haworth Medical Press.

Brown, S. (2002). Ethnic differences in pet attachment among students at an American school of veterinary medicine. *Society and Animals, 10,* 455-456.

Bunch, B. J., Lund, N. L., & Wiggins, F. K. (1983). Self-disclosure and perceive closeness in the development of group process. *Journal for Specialists in Group Work, May,* 59-65.

Bureau of Justice Statistics (2005a, July). *Substance dependence, abuse and treatment of jail inmates, 2002* (NCJ 209588). Washington DC: Bureau of Justice Statistics.

Bureau of Justice Statistics (2005b, July). *Criminal victimization in the United States, 2003, statistical tables* (NCJ207811). Washington DC: Bureau of Justice Statistics.

Burlingame, G. M., Fuhriman, A., & Johnson, J. E. (2001). Cohesion in group psychotherapy. *Psychotherapy, 38,* 373-384.

Butler, K. (2004). *Therapy Dogs Today.* Norman, OK: Funpuddle Publishing.

Cain, A. O. (1983). A study of pets in the family system. In A. H. Katcher & A. M. Beck (Eds.), *New perspectives on our lives with companion animals* (pp. 351-359). Philadelphia: University of Philadelphia.

Campbell, C., & Katcher, A. (1992). *Animal assisted therapy and dogs for autistic children: Quantitative and qualitative results.* Paper presented at the meeting of the 6th International Conference on Human Animal Interactions. Montreal, Canada.

Campbell-Berg, T. (2000). A case study using animal-assisted therapy to promote abstinence in a group of individuals who are recovering from chemical addictions. *Journal of Addictions Nursing, 12*(1), 31-35.

Carroll, K. M., Rounsaville, B. J., & Gawin, F. H. (1991). A comparative trial of psychotherapies for ambulatory cocaine abusers: Relapse prevention and interpersonal psychotherapy. *American Journal of Drug and Alcohol Abuse, 17,* 229-247.

Carroll, K. M., Rounsaville, B. J., & Keller, D. S. (1991). Relapse prevention strategies for the treatment of cocaine abuse. *American Journal of Drug and Alcohol Abuse, 17,* 248-265.

Catanzaro, T. E. (2003). Human-animal bond and primary prevention. *American Behavioral Scientist, 47*(1), 29-30.

Chafetz, M. E., Blane, H. T., Abram, H. S., Golner, J., Lacy, E., McCourt, W. F., et al. (1962). Establishing treatment relations with alcoholics. *Journal of Nervous and Mental Disease, 134,* 395-409.

Chandler, C. K. (2005). *Animal assisted therapy in counseling.* New York: Routledge.

Chinner, T. L., & Dalziel, F. R. (1991). An exploratory study on the viability and efficacy of a pet-facilitated therapy project within a hospice. *Journal of Palliative Care, 7*(4), 13-20.

Churchill, M., Safaoui, J., McCabe, B. W., & Baun, M. M. (1999). Using a therapy dog to alleviate the agitation and desocialization of people with Alzheimer's disease. *Journal of Psychosocial Nursing, 37*(4), 16-22.

Cieslak, E. J. (2001). *Animal-assisted therapy and the development of an early working alliance: The use of dogs in therapy with young adults.* Unpublished doctoral dissertation, The University of Wisconsin - Madison.

Cobb, S. (1976). Social support as a moderator of life stress. *Psychosomatic Medicine, 38,* 300-313.

Cohen, S. (1992). Stress, social support, and disorder. In H.O.F. Veiel & U. Baumann (Eds.), *The meaning and measurement of social support* (pp. 109-124). New York: Hemisphere.

Cohen, S. P. (2002). Can pets function as family members? *Western Journal of Nursing research, 24*(6), 621-638.

Cohen, S., Mermelstein, R., Karmarck, T., & Hoberman, H. M. (1985). Measuring the functional components of social support. In I. G. Sarason & B. R. Sarason (Eds.), *Social support: Theory, research and application* (pp. 73-94). Boston: Nijhoff.

Condoret, A. (1983). Speech and companion animals: Experience with normal and disturbed nursery school children. In A. H. Katcher & A. M. Beck (Eds.), *New perspectives on our lives with companion animals* (pp. 66-83). Philadelphia: University of Pennsylvania Press.

Connors, G. J., DiClemente, C. C., Carroll, K. M., Longabaugh, R., & Donoban, D. M. (1997). The therapeutic alliance and its relationship to alcoholism treatment participation and outcome. *Journal of Consulting and Clinical Psychology, 65*(4), 588-598.

Corson, S. A., & Corson, E. O. (1978). Pets as mediators for therapy. *Current Psychiatric Therapies, 18,* 195-205.

Covert, A. M., Whirren, A. P., Keith, J., & Nelson, C. (1985). Pets, early adolescents, and families. *Marriage and Family Review, 8,* 95-108.

Crits-Christoph, P., & Connolly Gibbons, M. B. (2003). Research developments on the therapeutic alliance in psychodynamic psychotherapy. *Psychoanalytic Inquiry, 23*(2), 332-349.

Crits-Christoph, P., Barnachie, K., Kurcias, J. S., & Beck, A. T., et al. (1991). Meta-analysis of therapist effects in psychotherapy outcome studies. *Psychotherapy Research, 1,* 81-91.

Cusack, O. (1988). *Pets and mental health.* New York: The Haworth Press, Inc.

Cuttler, R. B., & Fishbain, D. A. (2005). Are alcoholism treatments effective? the Project MATCH data. *BMC Public Health, 5,* 75.

Darabont, F. (1999). *The green mile* [Motion picture]. United States: Warner.

Davis, J. H. (1988). Animal-facilitated therapy in stress mediation. *Holistic Nursing Practice, 2*(3), 75-83.

Delta Society (1996). *Standards of Practice in Animal-Assisted Activities and Therapy.* Renton, WA: The Delta Society.

Delta Society. (2004). *About animal-assisted activities & animal-assisted therapy*. Retrieved October 29, 2004, from Delta Society Web Site: http://www.deltasociety.org/aboutaaat.htm

Delta Society. (2005). *Become a Pet Partner®.* Retrieved July 31, 2006, from The Delta Society Web Site: http://www.deltasociety.org/VolunteerAboutBecome.htm

Dembicki, D., & Anderson, J. (1996). Pet ownership may be a factor in the improved health of the elderly. *Journal of Nutrition for the Elderly, 15,* 15-31.

Department of Justice. (2002, January 22). *Department of Justice ADA Title III Regulation 28 CFR Part 36.* Retrieved November 14, 2004, from American Disabilities Act Web Site: http://www.usdoj.gov/crt/ada/reg3a.html

Dhooper, M. K. (2003). *Animal-assisted therapy: The effects of the presence of a trained therapy dog on group anxiety management training.* Unpublished doctoral dissertation, University of South Dakota.

Diclemente, C. C., Bellino, L. E., & Neavins, T. M. (1999). Motivation for change and alcoholism treatment. *Alcohol Research & Health, 23*(2), 86-92.

Doherty , W. J. (1995). *Soul Serarching*. New York: Basic Books.

Duncan, B. L., & Miller, S. D. (2000). *The heroic client: Doing client-directed outcome-informed therapy.* San Francisco: Jossey-Bass.

Duncan, B. L., Miller, S. D., Reynolds, L. R., Sparks, J. A., Claud, D. A., Brown, J., et al. (2004). *The session rating scale.* Retrieved January 10, 2005, from Talking Cure Web Site Web Site: www.talkingcure.com/documents/TheSRSArticle.doc

Duncan, B., Miller, S., & Sparks, J. (2004). *The heroic client: A revolutionary way to improve effectiveness through client directed, outcome informed therapy.* San Francisco: Jossey Bass.

Eames, V., & Roth, A. (2000). Patient attachment orientation and the early working alliance: A study of patient and therapist reports of alliance quality and ruptures. *Psychotherapy Research, 10,* 421-434.

Eckstein, D. (2000). The pet impact relationship inventory. *The Family Journal: Counseling Therapy for Couples and Families, 8,* 192-198.

Eddy, J., Hart, L. A., & Boltz, R. P. (1988). The effects of service dogs on social acknowledgements of people in wheelchairs. *Journal of Psychology, 1*(22), 39-44.

Edwards, N. E., & Beck, A. M. (2002). Animal-assisted therapy and nutrition in Alzheimer's disease. *Western Journal of Nursing Research, 24*(6), 697-712.

Fick, K. M. (1993). The influence of an animal on social interactions of nursing home residents in a group setting. *The American Journal of Occupational Therapy, 47,* 529-534.

Fine, A. (2006). *Handbook on animal-assisted therapy: Theoretical foundations and guidelines for practice* (2nd ed.). San Diego, CA: Academic Press.

Fine, A. H. (2000). *Handbook on animal-assisted therapy: Theoretical foundations and guidelines for practice.* San Diego, CA: Academic Press.

Fine, A. H., & Mio, J. S. (2006). The future of research, education, and clinical practice in the animal-human bond and animal-assisted therapy: Part C: the role of animal-assisted therapy in clinical practice: the importance of demonstrating empirically oriented psychotherapies. In A. Fine (Ed.), *Handbook on animal-assisted therapy: Theoretical foundations and guidelines for practice* (2nd ed., pp. 513-523). San Diego, CA: Academic Press.

Flores, P. J. (2004). *Addiction as an attachment disorder.* New York: Jason Aronson.

Folse, E. B., Minder, C. C., Aycock, M. J., & Santana, R T. (1994). Animal-assisted therapy and depression in adult college students. *Anthrozoos, 7*(3), 188-194.

Francis, G. (1976). Loneliness: Measuring the abstract. *International Journal of Nursing Studies, 13,* 153-160.

Frankenheimer, J. (1962). *Birdman of Alcatraz* [Motion picture]. United States: MGM.

Freud, S. (1913/1958). On beginning the treatment. In J. Strachey (Ed. and Trans.*) The standard edition of the complete psychological works of Sigmund Freud* (Vol. 12, 121-144). London: Hogarth Press.

Friedmann, E. (2000). The animal-human bond: Health and wellness. In A.H. Fine (Ed.), *Handbook on animal assisted therapy: Theoretical foundations and guidelines for practice* (pp. 41-58). San Diego, CA: Academic Press.

Friedmann, E. H., Katcher, A H., Lynch, J. J., & Thomas, S. A. (1980). Animal companions and one-year survival of patients after discharge from a coronary care unit. *Public Health Reports, 9*(5), 307-312.

Friedmann, E., & Thomas, S. A. (1995). Pet ownership, social support, and one-year survival after acute myocardial infarction in the cardiac arrhythmia suppression trial (CAST). *American Journal of Cardiology, 76,* 1213-1217.

Friedmann, E., Thomas, S. A., & Eddy, T. J. (2000). Companion animals and human health: Physical and cardiovascular influences. In A. L. Podberscek, E. S. Paul, & J. A. Serpell (Eds.), *Companion animals and us: Exploring the relationships between people and pets* (pp. 125-142). Cambridge, United Kingdom: Cambridge University.

Fuhriman, A., & Burlingame, G. M. (1990). Consistency of matter: A comparative analysis of individual and group process variables. *The Counseling Psychologist, 18*(1), 6-63.

Gammonley, J., Howie, A. R., Kirwin, S., Zaph, S. A., Frye, J., Freeman, G., et al. (1997). *Animal-assisted therapy: Therapeutic Interventions.* Renton, WA: Delta Society.

Garrity, T. F., & Stallones, L. (1998). Effects of pet contact. In C.C. Wilson and D.C. Turner (Ed.), *Companion animals in human health* (pp. 3-22). Thousand Oaks, CA: Sage.

Gaston, L., Marmar, C. R., Thompson, L. W., & Gallagher, D. (1991). Alliance prediction of outcome: Beyond in-treatment symptomatic change as psychotherapy progresses. *Psychotherapy Research, 1*(1), 104-112.

Gaylord, S. (1999). Alternative therapies and empowerment of older women. *Journal of Women and Aging, 11*(2-3), 9-47.

Gerbasi, K. (2004). *The Yerkes-Dodson Law and social facilitation: A predictive model for animal-assisted therapy effects.* Paper presented at the meeting of the Human-Animal Bond Initiative 2004 Conference. Lansing, MI.

Glasser, W. (1998). *Choice theory: A new psychology of personal freedom.* New York: Harper Perennial.

Goldkamp, J. S., White, M. D., & Robinson, J. B. (2002, April). *An honest chance: Findings from drug court participants focus groups in Brooklyn, Las Vegas, Miami, Portland, San Bernardino and Seattle*. Retrieved July 30, 2006, from United States Department of Justice Web Site: http://www.ncjrs.gov/html/bja/honestchance/

Gurman, A. S. (1977). The patient's perceptions of the therapeutic relationship. In A. S. Gurman & A. M. Razin (Eds.), *Effective psychotherapy* (pp. 503-545). New York: Pergamon.

Hamilton, C. E. (2000). Continuity and discontinuity of attachment from infancy through adolescence. *Child Development, 71,* 690-694.

Harley, L. P., & Schneider, M. (2004 March 25). *The effect of animal presence on perceptions of psychotherapists and disclosure in therapy*. Paper presented at the meeting of the Annual Student Research Conference. Toronto, Canada.

Harlow, H. F. (1958). The nature of love. *American Psychologist, 13,* 573-585.

Harris, M. D., Rinehart, J. M., & Gerstman, J. (1993). Animal-assisted therapy for the homebound elderly. *Holistic Nurse Practice, 8*(1), 27-37.

Hart, L. A. (2000). Psychosocial benefits of animal companionship. In A. H. Fine (Ed.), *Handbook on animal-assisted therapy: Theoretical foundations and guidelines for practice* (pp. 59-78). San Diego, CA: Academic Press.

Harvath, A. O., & Symonds, B. D. (1991). Relation between working alliance and outcome in psychotherapy: A meta-analysis. *Journal of Counseling Psychotherapy, 38,* 139-149.

Havassy, B. E., Hall, S. M., & Wasserman, D. A. (1991). Social support and relapse: Commonalities among alcoholics, opiates users, and cigarette smokers. *Addictive Behavior, 16,* 235-246.

Heath, D. T., & McKenry, P. C. (1989). Potential benefits of companion animals for self-care children. *Childhood Education, 65,* 311-314.

Heller, K., Swindle, R. W., & Dusenbury, L. (1986). Component social support processes: Comments and integration. *Journal of Consulting and Clinical Psychology, 54*(3), 466-470.

Henry, W. P. (1998). Science, politics, and the politics of science: The use and misuse of empirically validated treatment research. *Psychotherapy Research, 8,* 126-140.

Hester, R., Miller, W., Delaney, H., & Delaney, R. (November 1990). *Effectiveness of the community reinforcement approach.* Paper presented at the meeting of the 24th annual meeting o the Association for the Advancement of Behavior Therapy. San Francisco, CA.

Hines, L. M. (2003). Historical perspectives on the human-animal bond. *American Behavioral Scientist, 47*(1), 7-15.

Holcomb, R., & Meacham, M. (1989). Effectiveness of an animal-assisted therapy program in an inpatient psychiatric unit. *Anthrozoos, 2*(4), 259-264.

Holder, H., Cisler, Longabaugh, Stout, Treno, & Zweben (2000). Alcoholism treatment and medical care costs from Project MATCH. *Addiction, 95,* 999-1013.

Holmes, J. (1996). *Attachment, intimacy, autonomy. Using attachment theory in adult psychotherapy.* Northdale, NJ: Jason Aronson, Inc.

Hooker, S. D., Freeman, L. H., & Stewart, P. (2002). Pet therapy research: A historical review. *Holistic Nursing Practice, 17*(1), 17-23.

Hooker, S. D., Freeman, L. H., & Stewart, P. (2002). Pet therapy research: A historical review. *Holistic Nursing Practice, 17*(1), 17-23.

Hubble, M. A., Duncan, B. L., & Miller, S. D. (Eds.). (1999). *The heart and soul of change.* Washington D. C. American Psychological Association Press.

Hunt, S. J., Hart, L. A., & Gomulkiewicz, R. (1992). The role of small animals in social interactions between strangers. *Journal of Social Psychology, 32*(2), 245-256.

Hupcey, J. E. (1998). Clarifying the social support theory-research linkage. *Journal of Advanced Nursing, 27,* 1231-1241.

Jacobson, D. E. (1986). Types and timing of social support. *Journal of Health and Social Behavior, 27,* 250-264.

Johnson, R. A., & Meadows, R. L. (2002). Older Latinos, pets and health. *Western Journal of Nursing Research, 24*(6), 609-620.

Johnson, R. A., Meadows, R. L., Haubner, J. S., & Sevedge, K. (2003). Human-animal interaction. *American Behavioral Scientist, 47*(1), 55-69.

Johnson, R., Odendaal, J. & Meadows, R. (2002). Animal-assisted interventions research: Issues and answers. *Western Journal of Nursing Research, 24* (4), 422-440.

Jung, J. (1988). Social support providers: Why do they help? *Basic and Applied Social Psychology, 9*(2), 231-240.

Kanninen, K., Salo, J., & Punamaki, R. I. (2000). Attachment patterns and working alliance in trauma therapy for victims of political violence. *Psychotherapy Research, 10,* 435-449.

Katcher, A. H., & Friedmann, E. (1980). Potential health value of pet ownership. *Compendium of Continuing Education Practice, 2*(2), 117-121.

Katcher, A. H., Segal, H., & Beck, A. M. (1984). Comparison of contemplation and hypnosis for the reduction of anxiety and discomfort during dental surgery. *American Journal of Clinical Hypnosis, 27,* 14-21.

Katcher, A., & Wilkins, G. G. (1994). The use of animal assisted therapy and education with attention-deficit hyperactivity and conduct disorders. *InterActions, 12*(3), 1-5.

Kidd, A., & Kidd, R. (1986). Pet owner psychology: The human side of the bond. In P. Arkrow (Ed.), *The loving bond: Companion animals in the helping professions* (pp. 32-39). Saratoga, CA: R & E Publishers.

Koocher, G. P., & Keith-Spiegel, P. (1998). *Ethics in Psychology: Professional standards and cases* (2nd ed.). New York: Oxford University Press.

Kottler, J. A. (2000). *Doing Good* (Rev. ed.). Philadelphia: Brunner Rouledge.

Kruger, K. A., & Serpell, J. A. (2006). Animal-assisted interventions in mental health: Definitions and theoretical foundations. In A. Fine (Ed.), *Handbook on animal-assisted therapy: Theoretical foundations and guidelines for practice* (2nd ed., pp. 21-38). San Diego, CA: Academic Press.

Krupnick, J. L., Sotsky, S. M., Simmens, S., Moyher, J., Elkin, I., Watkins, J., & Pilkonis, P. A. (1996). The role of the therapeutic alliance in psychotherapy and pharmacotherapy outcome: Finding in the National Institute of Mental Health Treatment of Depression Collaborative Research Project. *Journal of Consulting and Clinical Psychology, 64,* 532-539.

Lafferty, P., Beutler, L. E., & Crago, M. (1989). Differences between more and less effective psychotherapists: A study of select therapist variables. *Journal of Consulting and Clinical Psychology, 57*(1), 76-80.

LaJoie, K. R. (2003). *An evaluation of the effectiveness of using animals in therapy.* Unpublished doctoral dissertation, Spalding University.

Lambert, M. J. (1992). Psychotherapy outcome research: Implications for integrative and eclectic theories. In J. C. Norcross & M. R. Goldfried (Eds.), *Handbook of psychotherapy integration* (pp. 94-129). New York: Basic Books.

Lambert, M. J., & Barley, D. E. (2001). Research summary on the therapeutic relationship and psychotherapy outcome. *Psychotherapy, 38,* 357-364.

Lambert, M. J., & Okiishi, J. C. (1997). The effects of the individual psychotherapist and implications for future research. *Clinical Psychology: Science and Practice, 4,* 66-75.

Law, S., & Scott, S. (1995). Tips for practitioners: Pet care: A vehicle for learning. *Focus on Autistic Behavior, 10*(2), 17-18.

Lee, D. R. (1983). Pet-therapy: Helping patients through troubled times. *California Veterinarian,* 24-40.

Lefkowitz, C. M. (2005). Animal-assisted prolonged exposure: A treatment for survivors of sexual assault suffering with posttraumatic stress disorder (Doctoral dissertation, Widener University, Institute for Graduate Clinical Psychology, 2005). *Dissertation Abstracts International, B 66/06,* 3415.

Levinson, B. M. (1966). Pets: A special technique in child psychotherapy. *National Humane Review, July-August,* 24-27.

Levinson, B. M. (1969). *Pet-oriented child psychotherapy.* Springfield, IL: Charles C. Thomas.

Levinson, B. M. (1972). *Pets and human development.* Springfield, IL: Charles C. Thomas.

Levinson, B. M. (1984). Human-companion animal therapy. *Journal of Contemporary Psychotherapy, 14*(2), 131-144.

Levinson, B. M. (1997). *Pet-Oriented Child Psychotherapy* (2nd ed.). Springfield, IL: Charles C. Thomas.

Lin, N. (1986). Conceptualizing social support. In N. Lin, A. Dean & W. Ensel (Eds.), *Social support life events and depression* (pp. 17-21). New York: Academic Press.

Lin, N., Simeone, R. S., Ensel, W. M., & Kuo, W. (1979). Social support, stressful life events and illness: a model and an empirical test. *Journal of Health and Social Behavior, 20*(1), 108-119.

Luborsky, L., Barber, J., Siqueland, L., Johnson, S., Najavits, L., Frank, A., et al. (1996). The Revised Helping Alliance Questionnaire (HAQ-II): Psychometric Properties. *The Journal of Psychotherapy Practice and Research, 5,* 260-271.

Luborsky, L., Rosenthal, R., Diguer, L., Andrusyna, T. P., Berman, J. S., Levitt, J. T., et al. (2002). The dodo bird verdict is alive and well-mostly. *Clinical Psychology: Science and Practice, 9*(1).

Main, M. (1996). Introduction to the special section on attachment and psychopathology: Part 2. Overview of the field of attachment. *Journal of Clinical and Counseling Psychology, 64,* 237-243.

Mallinckrodt, B., Bantt, D. L., & Coble, H. M. (1995). Attachment patterns in the psychotherapy relationship: Development of the Patient Attachment to Therapist Scale. *Journal of Counseling Psychology, 42,* 307-317.

Mallon, G. P. (1992). Utilization of animals as therapeutic adjuncts with children and youth: A review of the literature. *Child and Youth Care Forum, 21*(1), 53-67.

Mallon, G. P., Ross, S. B. Jr., & Ross, L. (2000). Designing and implementing animal-assisted therapy programs in health and mental health organizations. In A.H. Fine (Ed.), *Handbook on animal-assisted therapy* (pp. 115-127). San Diego, CA: Academic Press.

Marcus, L., & Marcus, E. (1998). Nosocomial zoonoses. *New England Journal of Medicine, 338*(11), 757-759.

Martin, D. J., Garske, J. P., & Davis, M. K. (2000). Relation of the therapeutic alliance with outcome and other variables: A meta-analytic review. *Journal of Consulting and Clinical Psychology, 68*(3), 438-450.

Marziali, E., Munroe-Blum, H., & McCleary, L. (1997). The contribution of group cohesion and group alliance to the outcome of group psychotherapy. *International Journal of Group Psychotherapy, 47,* 475-497.

Maslow, A. (1970). *Motivation and personality* (Rev. ed.). New York: Harper & Row.

McCrady, B. S., & Hay, W. (1987). Coping with problem drinking in the family. In J. Orford (Ed.), *Coping with disorder in the family* (pp. 86-116). London: Croom & Helm.

McCulloch, M. (1986). Animal-facilitated therapy: Overview and future direction. *National Forum, 66,* 19-24.

McKenzie, K. R. (1994). Group development. In A. Fuhriman & G. M. Burlingame (Eds.), *Handbook of group psychotherapy: An empirical and clinical synthesis* (pp. 223-268). New York: Wiley.

McNicholas, J., & Collis, G. M. (2000). Dogs as catalysts for social interactions: Robustness of the effect. *British Journal of psychology, 91,* 61-70.

Meier, P. S., Barrowclough, C., & Donmall, M. C. (2005). The role of the therapeutic alliance in the treatment of substance misuse: a critical review of the literature. *Addiction, 100*(3), 267-8.

Meier, P. S., Donmall, M. C., McElduff, P., Barrowclough, C., & Heller, R. F. (2006). The role of the early therapeutic alliance in predicting drug treatment dropout. *Drug & Alcohol Dependence, 83*(1), 57-64.

Melson, G. F. (1990). Studying children's attachment to their pets: A conceptual and methodological review. *Anthrozoos, 4*(2), 91-99.

Melson, G. F. (2001). *Why the wild things are: Animals in the lives of children.* Cambridge, MA: Harvard University Press.

Melson, G. F. (2003). Child development and the human-companion animal bond. *American Behavioralist Scientist, 47*(1), 31-39.

Melson, G. F., Peet, S., & Sparks, C. (1992). Children's attachment to their pets: Links to socioemotional development. *Children's Environments Quarterly, 8,* 55-65.

Merriam-Arduini, S. (2000). Evaluation of an experimental program designed to have a positive effect on adjudicated violent, incarcerated male juveniles age 12-25 in the state of Oregon. Unpublished doctoral dissertation, Pepperdine University.

Messent, P., & Serpell, J. (1981). A historical and biological view of the pet-owner interaction. In B. Fogle (Ed.), Interrelations between people and pets. Springfield: Charles C. Thomas.

Meyer, B., & Pilkonis, P. (2002). Attachment Style. In J. C. Norcross (Ed.), *Psychotherapy relationships that work* (pp. 367-382). New York: Oxford University Press.

Michaels, J.W., Blommel, J.M., Brocato, R.M., Linkous, R.A. and Rowe, J.S. (1982) Social facilitation and inhibition in a natural setting, *Replications in Social Psychology, 2,* 21-24

Miller, M., & Lago, D. (1990). The well-being of older women: The importance of pet and human relations. *Anthrozoos, 3,* 245-252.

Miller, W. (1999). *Enhancing motivation for change in substance abuse treatment: Treatment improvement protocol (TIP) series 35.* Rockville, MD: Substance Abuse and Mental Health Services Administration.

Miller, W. R., Rollnick, S., & Conforti, K. (2002). *Motivational Interviewing: Preparing people for change* (2nd ed.). New York: The Guilford Press.

Miller, W. R., Taylor, C. A., & West, J. C. (1980). Focused versus broad-spectrum behavior therapy for problem drinkers. *Journal of Consulting and Clinical Psychology, 48,* 590-601.

Mosher-Ashley, P. M., & Barrett, P. W. (1997). *A life worth living: Practical strategies for reducing depression in older adults.* Baltimore: Health Professionals Press.

Mugford, R. A., & McComisky, J. G. (1975). Some recent work on the psychotherapeutic value of cage birds with old people. In R. S. Anderson (Ed.), *Pet animals and society* (pp. 54-65). Baltimore: Williams and Wilkins.

Muschel, I. (1984). Pet therapy with terminal cancer patients. *Journal of Contemporary Social Work, 4*(10), 451-458.

Nagengast, D. E., Baun, M. M., Leibowitz, M. J., & Megel, M. (1993, October). *The effects of the presence of a companion animal on physiological and behavioral distress in children during a physical examination.* Paper presented at the meeting of the Delta Society 12th annual conference. St. Louis, MO.

Nagengast, S. L., Baun, M. M., Megel, M., & Leibowitz, J. M. (1997). The effects of the presence of a companion animal on physiological arousal and behavioral distress in children during a physical examination. *Journal of Pediatric Nursing, 12,* 323-330.

Nathanson, D. E. (1989). Using Atlantic bottlenose dolphins to increase cognition of mentally retarded children. In P. Loyibond and P. Wilson (Ed.), *Clinical and Abnormal Psychology* (pp. 233-242). North Holland: Elsevier.

Nathanson, D. E. (1998). Long-term effectiveness of dolphin-assisted therapy for children with severe disabilities. *Anthrozoos, 11*(1), 22-32.

Nathanson, D. E., & de Faria, S. (1994). Cognitive improvement of children in water with and without dolphins. *Anthrozoos, 6,* 17-29.

National Institutes of Drug Abuse (2000). *Principles of drug addiction treatment.* Washington, D.C.: NIDA.

National Institutes of Health, (NIH) (1988). *Health benefits of pets: Summary of working group.* Washington DC: U.S. Department of Health and Human Services.

National Institutes on Drug Abuse (1998, May). *The economic costs of alcohol and drug abuse in the United States, 1992.* (BKD265). Rockville, MD: National Clearinghouse for Alcohol and Drug Information.

Netting, F. E., Wilson, C. C., & New, J. C. (1987). The human-animal bond: Implications for proactive. *Social Work, 32*(1), 60-64.

Nightingale, F. (1860). *Notes on nursing: What it is and what it is not.* London: Harrison, 59, Pall Mall, Bookseller to the Queen.

Norcross, J. C. (2000). Empirically supported therapeutic relationships: A Division 29 Task Force. *Psychotherapy Bulletin, 35*(2), 2-4.

Norcross, J. C. (2002). *Psychotherapy relationships that work.* New York: Oxford University Press.

Norcross, J. C., & Beutler, L. E. (1997). Determining the therapeutic relationship of choice in brief therapy. In J. N. Butcher (Ed.), *Personality assessment in managed health care: A practitioner's guide* (pp. 42-60). New York: Oxford University Press.

Norris, P. A., Shinew, K. J., Chick, G., & Beck, A. M. (1999). Retirement, life satisfaction, and leisure services: The pet connection. *Journal of Park and Recreation Administration, 17*(2), 65-83.

Odendaal, C. (1999). *A physiological basis for animal-facilitated psychotherapy.* Unpublished doctoral dissertation, University of Pretoria, South Africa.

Odendaal, J. (2002). Pets and our mental health: The why, the and the how. New York: Vintage Press.

Odendaal, J. S. (2000). Animal-assisted therapy - Magic or medicine? *Journal of Psychosomatic Research, 49*(4), 275-280.

Orlinsky, D. E., Grawe, K., & Parks, B. K. (1994). Process and outcome in psychotherapy. In A. E. Bergin & S. L. Garfield (Eds.), *Handbook of psychotherapy and behavior change* (4th ed., pp. 270-276). New York: Wiley.

Orlinsky, D. E., Ronnestad, M. H., & Wilutzki, U. (2003). Fifty years of process-outcome research: Continuity and change. In M.J. Lambert (Ed.), *Bergin and Garfield's handbook of psychotherapy and behavioral change* (5th ed., pp. 307-390). New York: Wiley.

Pace, K. L. (1996). *The impact of animal-assisted therapy with an adolescent substance abuse population.* Unpublished doctoral dissertation, Rush University, College of Nursing.

Patronek, G. J., & Glickman, L. T. (1993). Pet ownership protects the risks and consequences of coronary heart disease. *Medical Hypotheses, 4*(0), 245-249.

Paul, E. S. (2000). Love of pets and love of people. In A. L. Podberscek, E. S. Paul & J. A. Serpell (Eds.), *Companion animals and us: Exploring the relationships between people and pets* (pp. 168-186). Cambridge, United Kingdom: Cambridge University Press.

Pence, M. J. (2005). Animal assisted therapy: A theoretical framework and case study (Doctoral dissertation, Regent University, 2005). *Dissertation Abstracts International, 3175627.*

Piazza, P. V., & Le Moal, M. (1998). Stress as a factor in addiction. In A. W. Graham & T. K. Schultz (Eds.), *Principles of Addiction Medicine* (pp. 83-93). Chevy Chase, MD: American Society of Addiction Medicine.

Pichot, T., & Coulter, M. (2006). *Pet-assisted brief therapy: A solution-focused approach.* Binghamton, New York: Haworth Press.

Pilisuk, M. (1982). Delivery of social support: the social inoculation. *American Journal of Orthopsychiatry, 52*(1), 20-31.

Poresky, R. H. (1990). The Young Children's Empathy Measure: Reliability, validity and effects of companion animal bonding. *Psychological Reports, 67,* 51-54.

Post-White, J., Kinney, M. E., Savik, K., Gau, J. B., Wilcox, C., & Lerner, I. (2003). Therapeutic massage and healing touch improve symptoms in cancer. *Integrative Cancer Therapies, 2*(4), 332-344.

Prescott, J. (2002). *Current usage and limitations of animal-assisted therapy.* Unpublished doctoral dissertation, California State University, Long Beach.

Prochaska, J. O., DiClemente, C. C., & Norcross, J. C. (1993). In search of how people change: Applications to addictive behaviors. *American Psychologist, 47,* 1102-1114.

Procidano, M. E., & Heller, K. (1983). Measures of perceived social support from friends and from family: Three validation studies. *American Journal of Community Psychology, 11*(1), 1-24.

Project Match Research Group (1997). Matching alcoholism treatments to client heterogeneity: Project MATCH posttreatment drinking outcomes. *Journal of Studies on Alcohol, 58*(1), 7-29.

Raina, P., Waltner-Toews, D., Bonnett, B., Woodward, C., & Abernathy, T. (1999). Influence of companion animals on the physical and psychological health of older people. *Journal of the American Geriatrics Society, 47,* 323-329.

Rajack, L. S. (1997). *Pets and human health: The influence of pets on cardiovascular and other aspects of owners' health.* Unpublished doctoral dissertation, University of Cambridge.

Raupp, C. D. (1997). Treasuring, trashing or terrorizing: Adult outcomes of childhood socialization about companion animals. *Society & Animals, 7*(2), 141-160.

Raupp, C. D., Barlow, M., & Oliver, J. A. (1997). Perceptions of family violence: Are companion animals in the picture? *Society & Animals, 5*(3), 219-237.

Redefer, L. A., & Goodman, J. F. (1989). Brief report: Pet-facilitated therapy with autistic children. *Journal of Autism and Developmental Disorders, 19,* 461-467.

Reichert, E. (1994). Play and animal-assisted therapy: A group-treatment model for sexually abused girls ages 9-13. *Family Therapy, 21*(1), 55-62.

Reichert, E. (1998). Individual counseling for sexually abused children: A role for animals and storytelling. *Child and Adolescent Social Work Journal, 15*(3), 177-185.

Reilly, R. M., Clark, W., & Shopshire, M. S. (1996). Anger management and PTSD: Engaging substance abuse patients in long-term treatment. *NCP Clinical Quarterly6, 6*(3). Retrieved July 31, 2006, from United States Department of Veterans Affairs Web Site: http://www.ncptsd.va.gov/publications/cq/v6/n3/reilly.html

Reite, M. (1989). Effects of touch on the immune system. In N. Gunzenhauser (Ed.), *Johnson & Johnson Pediatric Roundtable* 14: 22-31.

Renzi, K. A. (2005). An evaluation of the benefits of animal assisted therapy (Doctoral dissertation, The Chicago School of Professional Psychology, 2005). *Dissertation Abstracts International, 3177436.*

Robbins, S. B. (2006). Effect of comorbid psychiatric disorders on measures of group cohesion in substance abusers (Doctoral dissertation, Louisiana Technical University, 2006). *Dissertation Abstracts International, AA13184192.*

Robin, M., & ten Bensel, R. (1985). Pets and the socialization of children. *Marriage and Family Review, 8*(3), 63-78.

Rogers, C. (1951). *Client-centered therapy.* Boston: Houghton Mifflin.

Ross, S. B. (1983). The therapeutic use of animals with the handicapped. *International Child Welfare Review, 56,* 26-39.

Rynearson, E. K. (1978). Humans and pets and attachment. *British Journal of Psychiatry, 133,* 550-555.

SAMHSA (2000). *Substance abuse treatment for persons with child abuse and neglect issues: Treatment improvement protocol series 36* (BKD343). Washington, DC: U.S. Government Printing Office.

SAMHSA (2006a). *Discharges who left against professional advice: 2003* (Dasis Report Issue 28). Washington DC: Office of Applied Studies, Substance Abuse and Mental Health Services Administration.

SAMHSA (2006b). *Trends in substance abuse treatment admissions: 1993 and 2003* (The Dasis Report Issue 12, 2006). Washington DC: Office of Applied Studies, Substance Abuse and Mental Health Services Administration.

Sarason, S. (1995). *Caring and compassion in clinical practice.* Northvale, NJ: Jason Aronson.

Schantz, P. M. (1990). Reviews and research reports; presenting potential health hazards incidental to the use of pets in therapy. *Anthrozoos, 4*(1), 114-123.

Shumaker, S. A., & Brownell, A. (1984). Toward a theory of social support: Closing conceptual gaps. *Journal of Social Issues, 40*(1), 11-36.

Siegel, J. M. (1990). Stressful life events and use of physician services among the elderly: The moderating role of pet ownership. *Journal of Personality and Social Psychology, 58*(6), 1081-1086.

Siegel, J. M. (1993). Companion animals: In sickness and in health. *Journal of Social Issues, 49*(1), 157-167.

Siegel, J., Angulo, F., Detels, R., Wesch, J., & Mullen, A. (1999). AIDS diagnosis and depression in multicenter AIDS cohort study: The ameliorating impact of pet ownership. *AIDS Care, 11*(2), 157-170.

Simon, L. J. (1984). The pet trap: Negative effects of pet ownership on families and individuals. In R.K. Anderson, B. Hart & L. Hart (Eds.), *The pet connection* (pp. 226-240). Minneapolis: University of Minnesota Press.

Simpson, J. A., & Rholes, W. S. (1998). *Attachment theory and close relationships.* New York: Guilford.

Smith, J. E., & Meyers, R. J. (2004). *Motivating substance abusers to enter treatment.* New York: The Guilford Press.

Smith, M. L., & Glass, G. V. (1977). Meta-analysis of psychotherapy outcome studies. *American Psychologist, 32,* 752-760.

Spitz, R. (1950). Relevancy of direct infant observation. *Psychoanalytic Study Child, 5,* 66-73.

Stallones, L., Marx, M., Garrity, T., & Johnson, T. (1990). Pet ownership and attachment in relation to the health of U.S. adults, 21 to 64 years of age. *Anthrozoos, 4,* 100-112.

Steinglass, P. (1987). *alcoholic family.* New York: Basic Books.

Stewart, M. J. (1993). *Integrating social support in nursing.* Newbury Park, CA: Sage.

Strandberg, T. E. (2003). What is the most important component of blood pressure: systolic, diastolic or pulse pressure? *Current Opinion in Nephrology & Hypertension, 12*(3), 293-297.

Strauss, B. M. (2000). Attachment theory and psychotherapy research. *Psychotherapy Research, 10,* 381-389.

Strimple, E. O. (2003). A history of prison inmate-animal interaction programs. *The American Behavioral Scientist, 47*(1), 70-78.

Stroud, R. (1964). *Digest on the diseases of birds.* Neptune, NJ: TFH Publications.

Szymanski, E. M., & Parker, R. M. (2001). Epistemological and methodological issues in counseling. In D.C. Locke, J.E. Meyers, & E.L. Herr (Eds.), *The handbook of counseling* (pp. 455-466). Thousand Oaks, CA: Sage.

Taylor, E., Maser, S., Yee, J., & Gonzalez, S. M. (1993). Effect of animals on eye contact and vocalizations of elderly residents in a long-term care facility. *Physical and Occupational Therapy in Geriatrics, 11*(4), 61-71.

Templer, D. I., Salter, C. A., Baldwin, R., & Veleber, D. M. (1981). The construction of a pet attitude scale. *The Psychological Record, 31,* 343-348.

Terpin, J. L. (2004). Exploring the human-animal bond in an animal-assisted therapy program for at-risk youth (Doctoral dissertation, University of New England Graduate School, 2004). *Dissertation Abstracts International, 0419-4217.*

Thoits, P. A. (1982). Conceptual, methodological, and theoretical problems in studying social support as a buffer against life stress. *Journal of Health and Social Behavior, 23*(2), 145-159.

Thoits, P. A. (1985). Social support and psychological well-being: Theoretical possibilities. In I. G. Sarason & B. R. Sarason (Eds.), *Social support: theory, research and application* (pp. 51-72). Boston: Nijhoff.

Tilden, V. P., Nelson C. A. & May B. A. (1990). The IPR inventory: Development and psychometric characteristics. *Nursing Research, 39*(3), 337-343.

Tonigan, J. S., Miller, W. R., Chavez, R., Porter, N., Worth, V., Westphal, V., et al. (2004). *Project Match 10-year treatment outcome: Preliminary findings based on the Albuquerque Clinical Research Unit.* Retrieved January 10, 2005, from Center on Alcoholism, Substance Abuse, and Addictions (CASAA) Web Site: http://casaa.unm.edu/posters/project%20match%2010-year%20treatment%20outcome.pdf

Triebenbacher, S. L. (1998). Pets as transitional objects: Their role in children's emotional development. *Psychological Reports, 82*(1), 191-201.

Tschuschke, V., & Dies, R. R. (1994). Intensive analysis of therapeutic factors and outcome in long-term inpatient groups. *International Journal of Group Psychotherapy, 44,* 185-208.

Tuke, S. (1964). *Description of the Retreat.* London: Dawsons of Pall Mall.

Tyrrell, C. L., Dozier, M., Teague, G. B., & Fallot, R. D. (1999). Effective treatment relationships for persons with serious psychiatric disorders: The importance of attachment states of mind. *Journal of Consulting and Clinical Psychology, 59,* 725-733.

Vaux, A. (1992). Assessment of social support. In H. O. F. Veiel & U.Baumann (Eds.), *The meaning and measurement of social support* (pp. 193-216). New York: Hemisphere.

Vaux, A. (Ed.). (1988). *Social support - Theory, research and intervention.* New York: Praefer.

Verderber, S. (1991). Elderly persons' appraisal of animals in the residential environment. *Anthrozoos, 4,* 164-173.

Vidovic, V. V., Stetic, V. V., & Bratko, D. (1999). Pet ownership, type of pet and socio-emotional development of school children. *Anthrozoos, 12*(4), 211-217.

Walant, K. B. (1995). *Creating the capacity for attachment: Treating addictions and the alienated self.* Northvale, NJ: Jason Aronson Inc.

Walsh, P. G., & Mertin, P. G. (1996). The raining of pets as therapy dogs in a women's prison: A pilot study. *Anthrozoos, 7*(2), 124-128.

Walsh, P. G., Mertin, P. G., Verlander, D. F., & Pollard, C. F. (1995). The effects of a 'pets as therapy' dog on persons with dementia in a psychiatric ward. *Australian Occupational Therapy Journal, 42,* 161-166.

Wampold, B. E. (2001). *The great psychotherapy debate: Models, methods and findings.* Hillsdale, New Jersey: Lawrence Erlbaum.

Waters, E., Merrick, S., Treboux, D., Crowell, J., & Albersheim, L. (2000). Attachment security in infancy and early adulthood: A twenty-year longitudinal study. *Child Development, 71,* 684-689.

Weiss, R. (1974). The provision of social relationships. In Z. Rubin (Ed.), *Doing unto others* (pp. 17-26). Englewood Cliffs, New Jersey: Prentice-Hall.

Wells, D. L. (2004). The facilitation of social interactions by domestic dogs. *Anthrozoos, 17,* 340-352.

Wilson, C. (2006). The future of research, education, and clinical practice in animal-human bond and animal-assisted therapy:Part B: Human-animal interactions and Health: Best evidence and where we go from here. In A. Fine (Ed.), *Handbook on animal-assisted therapy: theoretical foundations and guidelines for practice* (2nd ed., pp. 499-512). San Diego, CA: Academic Press.

Wilson, C. C. (1991). The pet as an anxiolytic intervention. *The Journal of Nervous and Mental Disease, 179,* 482-489.

Wilson, C. C., & Barker, S. B. (2003). Challenges in designing human-animal interaction research. *American Behavioral Scientist, 47*(1), 16-28.

Woolverton, M. (1993). *An observational study on the responses of children to the presence of an animal during neuromuscular examinations.* Paper presented at the meeting of the First International Conference on Human-Animal Companionship. Mexico.

Yalom, I. D. (2005). *The Theory and Practice of Group Psychotherapy* (5th ed.). New York: Basic Books.

Yerkes, R. M., & Dodson, J. D. (1908). The relation of strength of stimulus to rapidity of habit-formation. *Journal of Comparative Neurology and Psychology, 18,* 459-482.

Young, F. W. (2004). Social Determinants, social supports and health: a critique. *Social Theory & Health, 2*(2), 142-152.

Zajonc, R. B. (1968) Attitudinal effects of mere exposure, *Journal of Personality and Social Psychology*, 9, Monograph supplement No. 2, Part 2.

Zisselman, M.; Rovner, B.; & Ferrie, P.(1996). A pet therapy intervention with geriatric psychiatry inpatients. *American Journal of Occupational Therapy, 50* (1), 47-51.

ABOUT THE AUTHOR

Dr. Martin Cortez Wesley is a Regional Academic Director and Assistant Professor with Lindsey Wilson College, School of Professional Counseling. He has been teaching at various levels for many years and operates his own private practice, New Leaf Center, in Bowling Green, Kentucky and online at *www.newleafctr.com*. He is also the vice-chair for the Kentucky Board of Licensed Professional Counselors.

Dr. Wesley specializes in marriage and family issues, depressive disorders, crisis services and addiction treatment. He lives in South Central Kentucky with his wife of 27 years. They enjoy time together in the new experience of an "empty nest" but regularly see and enjoy their three daughters, son-in-law and two grandchildren.

www.ingramcontent.com/pod-product-compliance
Lightning Source LLC
Chambersburg PA
CBHW070009300526
45794CB00001B/253